War

is a Failure of

Politics

A Christian's perspective

Henry Disney

PNEUMA SPRINGS PUBLISHING UK

First Published in 2015 by:
Pneuma Springs Publishing

War is a Failure of Politics
Copyright © 2015   Henry Disney
ISBN13: 9781782283881

British Library Cataloguing in Publication Data. A catalogue record for this book is available from the British Library.

Pneuma Springs Publishing
A Subsidiary of Pneuma Springs Ltd.
7 Groveherst Road, Dartford Kent, DA1 5JD.
E: admin@pneumasprings.co.uk
W: www.pneumasprings.co.uk

Dedication

In gratitude for the life of my wife
AUDREY DISNEY
22 January 1928 - 1 March 2012
(we were married on 23 November 1963)
and
for our children
TRUDIA, ADRIAN and RACHEL
and
our grandchildren
ALISTAIR, SAMANTHA, ZOE and MAX
for whom I hope for a more peaceful world

All royalties for the
ANGLICAN PACIFIST FELLOWSHIP
33 Glyneswood, Chinnor, Oxfordshire OX39 4JE
(apfpayne@btinternet.com   Charity number 209610)

Preface

I have been writing poetry since I was a teenager at school. My first collection was published 1963. Subsequent collections have appeared in 1982, 1995, 2004, 2006, 2009, 2011, 2012 and 2014. The 21st Century collections reproduced the poems from the previous thee collections. Full details of these are given at the back end of this volume. However, in each of these collections few of the poems were politically controversial.

This tenth collection gathers together in a single volume a selection of unashamedly political poems concerned with my deep antipathy to war. The criticism that I am too much down on Bush and Blair as opposed to the likes of Hitler, Sadam Hussein or today's promoters of war as an instrument of political change (such as Putin), is because the two Bs overtly declared themselves to be motivated by their Christian faith but in practice put their faith in the force of arms, despite Christ's rejection of violence.

Apart from the title poem, the poems are arranged in alphabetical order by title. The letters in brackets after their titles, e.g. (TL), refer to the particular collection of poems listed at the back. These collections include many that have been published previously. The details of their first public reading or publication are given in the relevant collection.

Henry Disney

'WAR IS A FAILURE OF POLITCS' (TL)

Today as apathy prevails
And cynics merely ladle scorn
On those who urge us heed the poor
Or those in need of helping hand;
Today when naked greed is praised
And ruthless competition rules,
It seems I'm out of line when I
Protest that way the world is run
Is truly mad beyond belief.
And when our leaders seek to earn
Their spurs by bombing lands beyond
Concern of common folk, I want
To yell that war is sign that those
Who advocate this way are blind
To truth that only those bereft
Of sense resort to force: it's sign
Of failure most profound: it's when
It's politics at end of road
Of reason's patient search for peace
Through tending wounds of conflicts caused
By slights perceived or half believed.
To see oneself with other's eyes,
However hard, depraved, they seem,
Is way to reconcile, to build
Anew. But no, we loose a load
Of bombs and missiles fired at cost
That's more than what's required to cure
The ills that caused offence before
The silly squabble ran away
With hope and common sense. So let
Us listen, let us talk instead.
It's better far than being dead!

AGAINST (CW)

He spits abusive words. He's pale
With rage. How dare I rant against
Both Bush and Blair for using force
Against Saddam Hussein, against
The Taliban and rest of gang.
"It's only right to fight against
The devil in disguise". But still
I'll criticise and speak against
The atavistic pair who waste
Our tax on arms to use against
Selected foes before they've tried
To understand their case against
The hubris, empire-minded cant.
To them the West's at war against
Beliefs they hold beyond dispute.
They know for sure what they're against.
Agreed Saddam was evil thug,
Whose own are best to rise against.
I must condemn both Bush and Blair.
They're blind to what they're up against.
I won't repent, I shan't recant,
I'm sure of what I'm up against;
But what I'm for is building peace.

ALL ASTRAY? (CW)

A rising tide of people day
By day augments the drain on rare
Resources, adds to toxic rain
That's making planet ill. We scare
Ourselves with future models meant
To help us plan for better way
To live our lives for good of all.
But still the poorest have no say.
Hubristic leaders go to war

Or arm fanatic fools who do
The same. It's all a game to make
A billion bucks or more. There's few
Who try to change the rules to make
For peace. Suggesting budget for
Defence be halved elicits groans
Of scorn. By helping hopeless more
We'd lessen calls for strife to gain
The rights they don't enjoy. Instead
We put our faith in weapons still –
But peaceless lie awake in bed.

ALOOF? (TL)

His mind was well above the norm,
His drive the same. His work, and that
Of team, was making gains that brought
Acclaim. Although I'd sometimes sat
Entranced by talks he gave I'm left
With nagging sense concerns of world
Had passed him by. As though if man,
Consumed by hate and rage, had hurled
A bomb at neighbour's home, he'd smiled
And said 'I'm glad it wasn't mine'
And carried on with daily tasks
Because for him his life was fine.
He's like a soldier off to war
Who thinks it's all a game with mates.
He gives no thought to fact their job's
To kill; despite the fierce debates
At home of whether cause is right.
But worse was Bush and Blair who, deaf
To call for pause, restraint, ignored
The awkward facts. They'd seemed as chef,
Who loses cool with fair complaints.
They labelled press and public all

As fools or knaves, who seized a chance
To paint them black, ignoring call
To re-assess the dodgy facts
On which they'd claimed to base their case.
It's blinkered folk obsessed by cause
Who live as though they're higher race.
And when in nasty mess of war
Confusion reigns, and little kids
And mums are killed by rocket gone
Astray, then like a school of squids
They hide the truth behind a cloud
Of murky spin and ink in sheet
Of lies for press. If only cash
That's spent on death were used to meet
The needs of those who only wish
To raise their children free from fear.
We long for leaders more restrained
Who know the price of war's too dear.
We need to understand the ire
That drives some men to kill and maim.
To place our trust in bombs and guns
Denies beliefs we both acclaim.

AMBUSHED (CW)

The greengage tree is dressed in white
Of blossoms luring early bees
And thought that summer fruits will bring
Us sweet delight. Too soon our hopes
Are smashed. A tardy frost destroyed
Our dream. The same had proved the fate
For whiff of spring when Tony Blair
Had entered Number 10. A blast
Of frozen views from Bush's mob
Diverted hopes of justice, peace
And patient work to understand

Islamic lands and ways beyond
A soundbite superficial view.
Besides, caldera Middle East
Erupts whenever West attempts
To shape the choice of those who rule
These lands of richest oil fields.
He failed to grasp that they perceive
Ourselves as foreign knights like those
Who joined crusades in bloody past.
He wouldn't heed the wiser words
Of those who disagreed with rush
To war. His good intents, along
With spin, were drowned in floods of tears
Of weeping mums abroad and here.
On history's page his name is black.

ASTRAY (TL)

While thousands march for peace today,
And polls suggest that most oppose
The foreign wars of Bush and Blair,
They both adopt a lofty pose
When asked to say what makes them think
They've got the right to interfere
In distant country's rotten ways.
The star by which they claim to steer
Is Gospel Christ proclaimed. Their acts
Derive from older books in which
The use of force is only means
To get one's way. The oil rich
They arm with guns and jets, despite
The fact they trample human rights.
The dispossessed and refugees
Are given crumbs and other slights.
They claim the moral heights with views
Revealing ignorance supreme

Of history's twists and turns. The birth
Of Israel used the means that seem
Are much the same as Hamas choose
Today. Their evil bomb, and one
Employed by Stern in past, both maim
And kill a mum; eclipsing sun
Of trust and hope for years to come.
The truth is death of child by shell
Astray is worst of crimes for which
Excuse is merely lie from hell.
The land's the same as when the Christ
Declined to back an armed revolt
Against oppressor Rome. His way
Is start by loving foe today.

BAMBOOZLED (CW)

A man with desire to be called
By title 'My Lord' was enthralled
When Blair with a grin
Declared it's no sin
A loan will ensure you're installed.

But when it emerged in the press
That Tony concocted this mess
He's swift to declare
This sordid affair
Is lie he intends to suppress.

It seems that his wish to be seen
As whiter than white was a screen
He thinks he's beyond
The need to respond
To critics who claim he's not clean.

The nation now knows that he lied
When Bush did insist he provide

Support for his war
Not sanctioned by law
They brush all protestors aside.

BETRAYAL (CW)

As tulips deck the stage of spring,
The snowdrops quit some weeks ago,
The birds are full of song, but not
For joy. Behind their hymns and psalms
The fight is on. Our lowly patch
Of real estate is battlefield
For smaller lots, the best of which
Are won by bullies on the make
Proclaiming rights they've self conferred.
They're like the Zionists in land
Of Palestine. They've seized the homes
From those who'd lived and died, and raised
Their kids since dawn of time, beside
The olive groves and orange trees
Their fathers planted long ago.
These deeds some Jews defend on grounds
Of need for ancient home away
From scenes of Holocaust, despite
They override the rights of those
Who share their truthful claim to be
Their brethren Semites sprung from same
Enduring stock. With crimes that stained
His every act, Sharon ignored
The lessons Hitler taught in tides
Of blood imagination fails
To comprehend. We then embraced
Desire of Jews to live in peace,
But since Sharon had pulled the plug
On sympathy, it faded fast,
Except with Bush the bully's mate.

BLACK AND WHITE LIES (CW)

(An incident on active service in Cyprus in 1958)

A sergeant Bill was friendless man whose soul had
shrunk
From long neglect as child. In fact, as sadist
warped
By hate and ill intent, he scorned the squad he led.
His bully ways had picked on Ken, a little man
With comic turn of phrase and jokes for every scene
Or small event. But Bill had crossed the bounds
and tried
To crush the will of Ken without relent until
A day he went too far. "I'll get you yet" was Ken's
Response he'd hissed between his teeth. A month
elapsed
When ambush struck and Ken was on the Bren that
day.
As mates had dived for ditch beside deceitful road
Then Ken had seized his chance. A burst in back of
beast
Curtailed his lashing tongue at last. When back at
base
The men in turn professed the bloke was killed by
foe.
The junior N.C.O. was left to last. The truth
He'd nearly grasped, but fell in line with lying
mates.
One night his sleepless conscience stirred and out it
poured
As we were on our own, on guard, in lull before
The dawn relieved our vigil's stint. "Perhaps it's
best
To let Bill's mum believe he died a hero's death".

BOYISH PRANK? (RE)

When Blair descended stairs today,
To take control, as he perceived,
Of Britain PLC, he groaned
At thought the Commons might object
To latest ill digested whim
That came to him in bath. And so
He chickened out and left the fray
To Leader of the House instead.
He flew about the land, to grin
And spin another speech replete
With clichéd good intent but short
On means to end. And then he goes
To school to let the press record
His easy way with kids who think
He's great for taking time to pose
With them at all. And boy who thought
He's fraud he just ignored, as law
Denies the vote to those of ten
Or less. At close of day he felt
A glow at having made a show.
But Britain PLC remained
The same as when he left his bath
With eager boy's desire to please
His favourite teacher once again.
All this would be a joke if Blair
Were only bloke in charge of shop
At end of street. But since he's not
He must be stopped - or else the world
Will blow apart with bombs of hate,
Resulting from the use of force
To implement his good intents.
He's never learned that throwing match
On box of fireworks is no laugh.

BRIDGING THE GAP (CW)

She views the world in black and white.
A stupid sin derived from mix
Of fear and ignorance profound.
There ain't a chance of easy fix
For most of problems man confronts.
It's always been that way we think.
There never was a golden age.
It's worse when anti science faith,
Of Moslem sects or Christian fools,
Upholds an ancient text; or else
Insists we follow crazy rules
Devised before compassion true
Religions teach became the norm.
When wed to politics one gets
A fast retreat from right reform
Designed to increase justice, build
A better deal for all. To loose
A pack of random violent acts
Is never right despite abuse
That's claimed to justify one's deeds.
But no amount of reason shifts
Her mental state, her rote of words
Devoid of sense. The gaping rifts
Between our views can not be bridged
Unless emotions undergo
A seismic change. It's solid facts
On which to build, and way to go
Is love unleashed, inspired by flow
Of same from God, its source and goal.
To quench its fires with dogmas long
Ago assigned to trash, with shoal
Of old taboos, or rites devoid
Of sense in light of what we know
Today, is plain perverse. But still
My own progress is sluggish slow.

BUSH WAR (RE)

Hussein may strut and bluff, but knows
His days in sun are nearly done.
But Bush desires to go to war
To banish Saddam's pile of bombs
Containing germs or toxins meant
To kill en masse, or even worse -
Atomic heads on rockets aimed
At Western towns. Bush little thinks
He puts at risk himself and friends.
Besides the Arab world would sure
Explode. It seems he's blind to fact
That he commands an arsenal
As vile. He cannot see he'd light
A fuse unleashing hell. It seems
He sees the world as black and white
With him to stand and fight on side
Of right. He cannot grasp there's those
Who see his country striding, head
In air, as empire armies in
The past. Without a mandate from
The peaceful nations far and wide
He's just a bully on the make.
He must desist for all our sakes
Before unleashing maddened beast,
Who'll trigger chain reactions far
And wide for years to come
And leave a trail of blameless blood.

BUSH WHACKED (RE)

His market stall was making way
At last. He'd build a house his wife
Would make a home. He'd plant some trees
Of favoured fruits beside a pool
And sit in shade to watch his son

At play. But all was empty dream
The day his conscript's order came.
Saddam required he march to war
Against Kuwait. When elder Bush
Opposed, he lost a leg from blast
Of bomb. At length his market stall
Was gaining ground again. His hopes
Were soon to be within his grasp.
But then the other Bush had spoiled
His plans. A missile went astray
And killed his son, his wife, his stall
And all his stock. A leaflet dropped
By plane declared – you're free at last.
The cost of lives is small in view
Of prize. – For him such lies enraged.
For him the name of Bush is used
To signify a curse as bad
As threats Saddam engaged. For him
His life has lost all shape and aim.
For him all leaders steal the dreams
From common folk, who only wish
For peace and chance to nurture schemes
For making world a place for joys.

CENTURY OF MY BIRTH (CO)

At start untutored men believed
In God and Queen and those in charge.
Bequeathed a widowed sovereign's curse
Of empire, led by fools whose birth,
Not worth, conferred their class, their God
Obscured by church embalmed by those
Who ruled, the solid structures cracked
Asunder when the Kaiser fumed
And decent men in droves were slain
In 'war to end all wars'. Their ends

Were planned behind the lines by clods
Of higher rank. So thanks to them
The common man awoke to fact
That he knew better than the toffs
The score upon the ground where death
And life engaged in games of dice.
Meanwhile from untried gospel's dregs
Had risen godless creeds. But Marx,
Usurped by Lenin's ruthless will,
Became a curse that Stalin forged
Into machine whose fuel was fear
And product grief. Its only prize
Was bloody end to Hitler's Reich.
A case of wielding ugly beast
To crush another of its kin.

These bleeding rounds of senseless war
Unleashed a woman's right to choose,
Destroyed the ancient class divides.
The empty plinths were soon purloined
By self-made men and media names -
To benefit of comic turns
And cartoon jokes. New energies
Emerged in every walk of life;
And folk from other lands enriched
Our lives, despite the bile of those
Whom Hitler's crimes had left unmoved.
Not all the dinosaurs had died.

By end we surfed the internet
At will. Awash with facts and grot
Galore, we fail to find a clue
To goal of life. The light eludes
The mass who want to know the truth
Without a spin or sceptic's scorn.
The grand advance of science marred
By evil misapplications

And childish claims to other fields
Long ploughed by scholars of renown.
The politicians now are clowns
As party whips ensure they're dumb.

Since science showed us nature's way
To be destruction now - to build
Anew, in ceaseless rounds, it's seemed
We're merely playthings in a plot
From which we fear there's no escape.
As long as bombs and rapes, and frauds,
Abusing kids, and buying goods
Produced by those on paltry wage,
Are so the norm we feel no rage,
The world will merely turn to watch
Two teams engage in media quiz
Or monied sports gift-wrapped in hype.

Despite the wish of common man
To live in peace, it seems we're cursed
By those who vest their hopes in arms.
Until the teenage tantrums once
Again erupt in blows and tears,
The disillusioned young instead
Pursue escapes - in wealth, in dreams
As stars of sport or pop, in balm
Of lost beliefs exhumed from graves
Despite repellent stench that old
Hypotheses long dead exude.
Or else they turn to drugs or drink,
Or mindless games of make believe
On screens of VDUs where most
Are set in future worlds at war
Or corny interchange of men
With other forms of life to make
Biologists convulse or choke.

But still there's some impelled to search
For peace and justice in our day.
In this they join the covert ranks
Of those whom Christ invites to be
Compassion's yeast and seeds of joy.
It's still his Kingdom's call, without
The screen of dogmas daft, that points
Our way in this life - and beyond.
I journey on this road in hope,
For none has found a better route.

'COLLATERAL DAMAGE' (CW)
(Aftermath of 11 September 2001)

'Revenge is sweet' the adage snarls,
'We must avenge the wrong those planes
Inflicted when they flew, with ill
Intent and certain death, to kill
Those thousands unaware their lives
Were done'. We rage at means they chose
To force their bloody cause to top
Of headlined page of every paper sold
Across the globe. So now a thirst
To even score, and more, prevents
Our atavistic leaders pause
To ask themselves if means they use
To reach their goal are not as black
As those employed by terror gangs.
And so the bombs and missiles rain
Remorseless storm. The fact that one
In five have gone astray is 'just
A risk of war'. A mother finds
Her child is dead and home is blown
Asunder. 'Just a price to pay
For freedom' drones a stony faced,
Bemedalled, man from Pentagon.

When duty's day is done he finds
His car's a pile of scrap, his wife's
Dismembered by a hidden bomb
Designed to force a point of view
That's held as strongly as his own.
So now his wrath ensures his heart
Is coldly rigid with resolve
To have revenge - till death is king.

'COMPARE AND CONTRAST' (TL)

When Labour watered down our hopes,
For world not geared to feeding greed
Of those who trade in shares, it strained
Belief in fairer deals for those
Whose daily lives are fight to just
To stay alive. So when pretence
Is thrown aside and Blair decides
His party's not for peace but war,
In Kosovo, Iraq, where next?,
Is way to leave his mark on page
Of time's relentless scroll of deeds
Of folly done in name of good
To be achieved by force alone,
It's then my faith in Labour's dreams
Were stilled at last. By then desire
To stay in charge became the guide.
It's like a teenage boy resolved
To tame his lust but can't resist
The lure of lurid magazines.
It's only votes of those whose views
Reflect an ignorance supreme
Whose voice prevails. To give a lead
Is not in vogue as focus groups
Must now decide. As those who feel
Compassion's twinge complain, the spin

Now swamps their moans with frothy words,
Like firemen overwhelming blaze
With blanket foam. While Blair resorts
To ancient ways to shape the world,
I will not buy his specious screeds.
I spurn his claims. The contrast Christ
Commends is stark. His way is that
Of silent yeast transforming dough.
No polls are used to gauge the mood
Of mob before he chose the words
He wished to preach. He spoke his mind
With fearless unconcern for what
The men of self importance thought.
His Word is still at work today
For those who put their faith in grace.

CONSCRIPTED (CO)

The tele screen erupts with scene
Of tanks in desert sand at night,
As flares and mortar rounds explode
In thumping show of fairy lights.
For youth beneath that distant show
It's not such fun. He sees his mate
Is killed and then he's hit by chunk
Of metal in his guts. The pain
Is worse than hell on earth. He pleads
For swift relief. He never wished
To join this army, now in full
Retreat. He'd dreamed of work amongst
The children needing doctor's skill.
His training due was stalled when post
Had come with orders long he'd feared.
So now he lies in helpless pain
Awaiting aid. Another rain
Of bombs now drives his fellows back.

At length some nervous yanks appear.
They tend his wounds. They also talk
Of whole affair as bloody mess.
They wish they'd stayed at home and Bush
Had lost to Gore, as all now know
He really did. He shares their hate
Of cruel beast Saddam. How come
Both ballot box and naked force
Produced a pair so steeped in blood?
How come this pair of clowns, whose pasts
Are stained by scandal's taint, had come
To be in charge? They both aspired
To glowing place on history's page,
But both will be forgot except
As cause of fractured peace and pain.
For both, the middens scholars rake
Will be their end abode. Their names
Will be invoked to caution child
Who strays or used to vent one's spleen.

COSTLY CAUSE (MC)

Without a glance we pass the bronze
Of Empire general riding high
Above the snarl of traffic's roar.
His long forgotten war is best
Dismissed from minds of we who now
Regret his costly cause, the slaves
We sold across the seas, the arms
That some purvey to tyrants still.
Despite this legacy of sin,
Our nation's now a glory mix
Of diverse peoples, cultures, not
To mention arts, cuisine, and crumbs
Of foreign words enriching ours.
So let's rejoice in mongrel race

Whose common theme is love of all
Those freedoms slowly won from kings
And despot barons, including right
To lampoon those who rule today.
Let's celebrate our right to be
Ourselves, in dress, in speech, in way
We think, eccentric pastimes, care
For injured pets or oiled swans
That other folk might put to death
To end their pain. Rejoice we can
Complain with hope we'll get redress
In end. We want the rogues and cheats
Removed, but chafe at petty rules.
We're all within both puritan
And libertine in civil wars
Between our heads and feeling hearts.

DELUDING LIE (RE)

I'm immunised against desire
For war by active service in
My youth. And while I know I saved
Some lives, the larger problem still
Remained. And yet it's once a year
I wear my medal still, but not
With pride. I mourn the waste of life,
The injured children, seeds of hate
And fractured trust that still persists.
The use of force is seldom neat.
It tends to bring just brief reprieve
From fear and prejudice. The peace
We all desire cannot be bought
By use of arms, which just suppress
The flames of rage for while. Beneath
The surface glowing coals persist
Abiding time until we sleep.

But lesson's never learned, as when
With groans we witnessed once again
As Bush and Blair, with good intents,
Had blundered into swamp of feuds
Suppressed by Saddam's rule of bleak
Iraq, where blood is spilled without
Remorse as routine daily game.
Equating might with right has been
Deluding lie we still espouse,
Despite persistent cries of those
Who suffer still and urge a halt.
But atavistic Blair was deaf,
Along with Bush's gang of crooks.

DELUSIONS (TL)

As woman on the brink of state
Of mental 9/11 tries
To hide her inner tumble-dry
Frenetic spin, obscures with lies
Her fears, it seems a speech by Bush
Conceals behind the jaunty grin
A kid who's caught at nicking sweets.
He's quick to point to specks of sin
In other's eyes but fails to see
The splintered planks that fill his own.
He's spilled the jug of cream but
Won't admit it's him. He's sown
The seeds of dire revenge but blames
Al Qaeda's evil plan to rule
The West. He worships god of war
But claims a Christian view. The fool
Selects the texts from books before
The Gospel's light to underline
His prior views derived from lust
For money's lure, his sacred wine

Along with bread of being in
Control, or so he thinks. The way
Of cross and patient love has passed
Him by. The servant king, who may
Forgive the worst offence, is not
A model he applies. Assent
To doctrines long since lost in fog
Of abstract froth reveals extent
Of ignorance supreme. His lack
Of doubt recalls deluding quack.

DESERTION (RE)

He walks alone along the street
With pavements polished black by rain,
While puddles dodge the searching lights,
While heavy load is twisting gait.
He flees this day from friends whose hate
Consumes their boyhood trust with bombs.
They spurn his call for compromise,
They laugh to scorn his pleas for quiet
Attempts to woo the minds and hearts
Of muddled, thoughtless men who strive
In vain to use the law to calm
The rage of folk whose faith is cold.
Their anger glowed when he refused
To carry guns to secret lair.
So now he must be on the run,
Despite his girl, who begs him stay.
They'd joked when he on seat had sighed
To watch this pretty lass who'd come
His way without a care or dread
To mar her jaunty smile and hair
That taunted sun with gleams of fire.
But now she shrugs her shoulders once,
Before she writes him off as dunce.

His former mates with jeers and sneers
Dismiss his dreams as mental cramp.
But silent as the rising damp
His light is quenching people's fears.

DETACHED (RE)

The window frames a scene of green
Delight. A cedar stands above
The passing years with quiet disdain.
A weeping poplar trails the tips
Of curtained tresses gently on
The carpet lawn where blackbirds search
For tardy worms. A dainty birch,
In constant dance of leaves in sun,
Is as a Japanese design
On silk. A sudden breeze as clouds
Of menace grey disturb the calm.
A lightning flash, a growl afar
Announces storm is on its way.
And soon the trees are tossed and torn
In rage of wind and hurtling hail,
Whose bouncing stones become a spread
Of winter scene on summer's dream.
Within an hour the sun returns
And slowly steaming, gleaming drops
Begin to shrink and birds resume
Their constant search for food for young
In world renewed as thunder moves
Beyond our range to ravage towns
Away to north. The aftermath
Of war is thus, before the clouds
Of folly gather overseas
And threaten once again our peace.
But still the cedar stands aloof.

DISSENTING RAGE (CW)

A sense of impotence in face
Of Blair and Bush intent on war
Has stoked a sense of rage that won't
Subside. It means returning once
Again to gnawing theme in vain
Attempt to cleanse my mind. This grit
Could never form a pearl as long
As blooded hands prolonged attempts
To shape the world by force of arms.
They can't perceive themselves as gang
Of bullies on rampage. It seems
They came to think their silly spin
Was truth indeed, instead of lies
And black deceit. Our sense of shame
At what they'd launched on our behalf
Without consent has left us cold,
Bereft of sense our nation stands
For common good and peace abroad.
Instead we're branded evil thugs
Pursuing selfish goals alone.
But I for one dissent. It's time
To make amends, to turn our backs
On pair of well-intentioned fools
Who saw themselves as gallant knights
Crusading once again for rights.

DISTORTION (CW3)

A parcel neatly sealed with tape,
Addressed in shaky capitals,
Arrived today. I wondered if
It's safe. Perhaps it's bomb or pack
Of poison powder meant to kill.
I take it into garden, where
With care I slice away one end.

I then extract the inner sheath
Until it slips to lawn. It's then
I laugh aloud, for there revealed,
All neatly wrapped, is piece of cake
From friend who's just been wed abroad.
It seems that Bush and Blair have made
he world a place of fear that blights
Our minds beneath the surface calm
We still display. In truth the risk
Is so remote it's less than chance
Of accident on way to work
Each day. Perhaps inducing fear
Is ploy to make us all accept
Erosion, bit by bit, of rights
We've slowly won since John and Charles
The First had tried to treat the mass
With arrogant contempt. Today
Our leaders need our votes, but then
They want us docile, kept in check
By keeping us in dark behind
A spin of doctored flood of facts
That float upon the Internet
To make us think we're in the know.

DIVISIONS (RE)

I find it strange you claim to know
That prose and poetry never meet.
You seem to see them ever ranged
As rival teams on football field.
But I have savoured many bowls
Of prose that far exceed some plates
Of rhyming verse in terms of taste
Of pure delight and beauty raised
Beyond the norm of idle talk.
In practice writing either moves

Or leaves us cold. The form employed
Is neither here nor there. I read
For pleasure what is served, as long
As author doesn't try to fool
With hash of jumbled sense in place
Of real desire to share with me
Whatever made them want to write.
The sieves of time will save what's good.
I only wish that Ulster folk
Would come to see the same is true
Of what divides their tribes is just
The dregs of past disputes that now
Are dead as clash that caused the fall
Of Troy or Caesar's Gallic wars.
It's time we judged each piece of prose
Or verse, or person on their own
Without regard to genre or tribe.

DOUBLE STANDARDS (RE)

In youth I hunted terror gangs
In Cyprus, land of dreams that should
Have been a taste of paradise.
We exercised the greatest care
To not abuse our naked force,
Avoiding harm to mums and kids
And those attending vines, despite
The fact we couldn't tell the good
From bad amongst the men who sipped
Their tiny cups of coffee thick
With sludge of grounds. Our soldiers sent
To Ulster's troubled streets were same.
We fought the men who lived by gun
And death with cool restraint, despite
It meant our task was thus constrained.
We'd search each nook of suspect house,

While seething owners stood outside
Beneath the watchful gaze of dog
That's trained to kill; but kids we sat
Along a wall and gave them sweets!
Both Bush and Blair are not deterred
By risk of children's deaths. They launch
Their crudely aimed grenades and shells.
Iraqi mums and Afghan babes
Are zapped as part of cost, as words
Of easy 'deep regret' pollute
Our tele screens. The rubbled homes
Are stark reminder tactics used
Are not what we'd accept at home
As means to end that's justified.

DUXFORD IMPERIAL WAR MUSEUM (CW)

Our trip with lovely daughter's kids
To Duxford's sheds of planes and tanks,
Of guns and other tools of war,
Had subtext urging ceaseless thanks
For peace secured by means of all
This kit. As children learned a lot
From clever, even elegant,
Designs displayed, one soon forgot
Obscene amounts of cash, of work,
Creative skills were just employed
To better zap the other side
Before ourselves could be destroyed.
Resources spent could conquer want
For many still deprived of dream
Of daily bread. The title irks.
Recall of empire, I would deem
As out of place as time when slaves
Provided wealth for lavish homes
The National Trust now owns with pride.

The shop is stocked with many tomes
And tacky toys that take delight,
One feels, in war; as though it's all
A children's game.   Resort to force
To foster peace is not a brawl
Between opposing gung-ho knights.
Today it's mothers, children most
At risk from missiles, bombs, the rest
Of ghastly ordnance here they boast
Was fastest or the best for task
Of wreaking havoc on the foe.
Recoil from war is reinforced
By all this slick design on show.
If only all those able minds
Had planted wisdom seeds that grew
To give us lasting peace. Instead
This ugly beauty, old and new,
Confirms our need to heed the voice
Of Christ from long ago to try
To love our foes, placate their fears,
Address complaints. If not we die.
The urge to seek revenge for wrongs
Perceived becomes as drug to drain
Concern, destroying trust, until
Our fears and sense or anger gain
Control and overwhelm desire
For seeking calm and common cause.
It's those who try to mend esteem
Who should deserve the most applause.
And yet to witness pure delight
Of grandson's eager eye for ace
Displays has made our day. We pray
He'll never join the fighting race.
My lasting hate of war derives
From time in youth, as soldier sent
To play a minor part in fight
Against the vicious gang who rent

Apart idyllic Cyprus all
For nowt. I honour those who served
In thankless game restoring peace,
With hope it might be long preserved.

EVIDENCE-BASED PRESCRIPTIONS (CW)

The greatest change to cures employed
By doctors since the ancient Greeks
Has been their testing, double blind,
Before prescribed. The best when shrieks
Of pain are brought to heel by pills
We know are safe to use. And yet
Our politicians still believe
That war is certain way to set
The world aright, in spite of shoals
Of facts on history's page that show
That's not the case. Despite a cause
Is right, excess of force may sow
The seeds of bitter thirst for sweet
Revenge to haunt our dreams, inflame
Our fears. Unless a peace is built
On trust it's only pause in game
By which we share in villain's guilt.

EVOLUTION (RE)

The tooth and claw, the probe and sting,
The snare, the web, the cunning trap,
The serpent's strike, the swoop of hawk
Embroider life with diverse forms.
The beauty seen in perfect pounce
Redeems the fearsome flow of blood.
It seems the birth of love in man
Has sprung from brain designed to kill.
But now his need for flesh is tamed

He turns to hunting self instead -
Or else denies his brother's right
To run his race another way.
He slowly nails him to a cross,
Or else he slams the door on maid
Who seeks a place to cradle Christ,
Whose word of peace dethrones our past,
Whose grasp of truth will pluck us clean.

FAITH UNDER FIRE (MC)
(On active service in Cyprus in 1958, when
terrorism was sponsored by a church and a cat was
mistaken for a man at night)

Behold these hills smothered with rich
Profusion of wild flowers, see
Spring's rainbow wash overwhelm
These stone-strewn slopes with gentle tide.
At dusk perceive the sinking sun
Suck colour from the anaemic
Land as, blood-gorged, it had begun
To disappear - while we lie lost
Within the circularity
Of ourselves and despair.
And now the moon descends while weird
Resounding calls of Scops owls give
Eerie overtones to the black
Depths of expectancy. Behold!
Revolving slowly by that dark
And silent stony gorge, whose sill
Is overhung by writhing stems
Which taunt our straining eyes with doubts,
Does Judas hang beneath that tree?
Are we the absent crowd who jeer
His end, disturb his anguished
Thoughts? Did he grasp Jesus' mission

As he died, while wind creaked the branch,
Flies walked his empty expression?
It's thus I muse until the crack
Of a rifle, or the jittery
Rattle of bren-fire, brings us back
Intermittently to the now.

Grenades at tiny kids whose shrieks
Echo in vain – the homemade bombs -
Pierced bleeding guts of pregnant wives -
The booby-traps on corpse - No remorse
When performed for the cause. And we,
Despite our selfless comradeship,
With fierce festering fury sink -
Reaching beastial depths; irate,
Licentious soldiery who rape
Defenceless virgins; filch; torture
As ordered, or unauthorized.

For now a headline traps our gaze.
A complacent politician's
Paltry euphemisms now crawl
From the mourning black slabs of black,
Black type being fed by Fleet Street
To the indifferent and the damned.
My angry thoughts renew their quest
For reasons why poor Judas failed.
His corpse now slowly sways in mind,
Repugnant as some trendy priest
Who eschews the Way of the Cross
With talk of "call to freedom's fight
Which claims support from us at least."

A sudden gust hurls a strange cry
For mercy down the gorge of death.
A soft echo comes sighing back
"There, but for the grace of the Lord,

Goes each saint. Weep for Judas, weep.
With contrition water the land."
A soft pale shape seeped into view.
At once I'm straining every nerve.
Within me warred a deep desire
To kill, compassion, and a fear
That I would funk it when obliged
To shoot. All is opaque. The crack
Of the rifle in my hands brings back
My churning fears and thoughts to time;
To view a silent cat whose life
Is stopped, whose sudden death augments
The stream of blood with which a church
Astray impedes the love of Christ.
Again I ask - Did Judas find his peace?
And is the gilded cross above
Still lit by springtime's gentle sun?

I hear a silent shriek in my head.
I see the albatross past return
To the deep. The sky rends. Past is past,
And seems strangely detached, somewhere in
which
I seem no more involved. Childlike
I now behold the world with new eyes
And find I'm exiled no longer
From mankind - despite a strangely sacred,
Sceptical vision. I recall
The splendour and scent of Cyprus
Blossoms in spring. I hear mountain
Streams whisper in my ears; sense Christ's
Love welling forth in the world.
Perceive Christ's love beneath the blood
And beauty. But as in a dream
Which one partly controls, I shrink
From an unholy church and all
Its accretions; I rebound, I

Contrive to circumnavigate
Its monstrous, twisted edifice.

Having left that building far
Behind, the cross on its burnished
Dome still casts upon living past
Its ever lengthening shadow.
On glancing back, there remains
Only the cross - haloed by Light.
And now I see the same ahead
As guiding star of faithful church.

FILM SPECTACULAR (CW)

We watched a film that's highly praised,
But soon attention wandered wild.
The constant battles, fought with swords
And spears and arrows raining down,
Began to pall. Despite the theme
Of good defeating evil in
The end, the violence, blood and sheer
Delight in horror drained all sense
Of moral gain. Besides the pace
Was slowed by stretching out the scenes
Of death. Each image conjured forth
By technocrats who fused some film
Of living actors, settings real
And those imagination paints,
Along with figures nightmares spawn,
Is truly worth the praise it gains.
But overall the film's a flop.
The virtual beasts embody some
We know today with parts from myth
Or dinosaurs. The men recall
Icelandic sagas, while the tale
Is science fiction froth of wars

Between the beings future sends
From distant worlds in outer space.
The millions spent, the software skills
Employed, have not achieved the depths
A simple sonnet can when words
Alone are used to feed our souls.

FOR WHAT DID THEY DIE? (CW)

A sniper's burst of hateful fire
Has stained the street below. Today
Recall that dreadful hour when death,
In plucking passer by, had seized
Her baby's life for play, and lodged
A bullet in her spine and killed
Her lower half for life and left
Her helpless in a chair - bereft.

Recall the death of gunman's mate
Who killed himself with homemade bomb
Intended first for soldier's bar.
Recall his twisting reach for world
Of justice, rights and human scale.
He longed for brotherhood of man
But scorned the road of love and hope
And felled himself with his own rope.

This bread and wine recall a man
Whose death has lit a path through life
With vision bright, whose Kingdom's joy
Is not enforced by bomb or hate.
Through patient tears he sees his flock
His message twist, destroying peace.
He walks the way of cross and shame
To keep alive his Easter flame.

FUTILE OPERATION (CW)

A youth went forth to war without
A qualm. Indeed he thought it great
To go abroad with mates with whom
He relished varied sports and drink
At close of day. At night he dreamed
Returning hero to his home -
His wound would bleed, but pain was not
A feature felt in fancied scene.
As days got rough he laughed and joked
To keep their spirits up, until
The time he stepped on mine. So now
He's wheelchair bound and out of work.
It's now he starts to wonder why
The politician's thought that war
Would solve the conflict that arose.
It's plain it's merely sown a load
Of hate as seed of bitter strife
To come. Whoever wins will lose
The right to claim esteem as peace
Erodes. The cause of clash remains,
And 'compromise' is now a word
Assigned to bin of crippled hopes.
A tiny nodule may have been
Excised by surgeon's knife. But now
Relapse has spread disease beyond
The scar to every part, as rage
Is rising to the boil below
Apparent calm, as weasel words
Become a pastime that's the norm.
The war's postponed a larger storm.

GAMBLE (RE)

A spokesman, deadpan, gave reply
'Perhaps a half a million may

Be final score who'll lose their lives
In bid to oust Saddam. The price
Is high but think of peace restored
As prize'. I wonder what his tune
Would be if told his wife and son
Had drawn the shortest straw and now
Will die as part of deal. I doubt
He'd think the story real. To him
The deaths he plots are merely points
On graph, or abstract risks in game
That's played on map of world in place
Of board with dice and plastic men.
·To me demise of single child
From bomb that goes astray is crime
Beyond repair. I feel despair
At thought of decent men detached
To point when people only count
As numbers weighed against the costs
Of other ways they guess could be,
If worst of fears were ever true.
I'm not a counter in a pile
That's placed before the wheel is spun.
I can't condone such games of risk.
I'd rather muddle on in hope
That talks will inch our way to peace.

GONE ASTRAY (TL)

There's not a whiff of wind or sound
As gentle mist begins to lift.
There's not a hint of day before
When death had struck from sky as swift
As stoop of hawk, in form of bomb
Intended for a nearby bridge
But, as the Bush assault was wont,
Had missed. Retreating plane was midge,

A fading speck, all unaware
It killed my wife and baby girl.
Was this a price I had to pay
For right to vote? I want to hurl
Abuse, in grief, at Tony Blair,
Whose actor's words of feigned regret
Are worse than silent tears. What made
Him think we wanted him to set
Our country right? What hubris drives
Him in belief he's called to put
The world aright? His every move
Is like a kid who puts his foot
On precious plant when chasing ball
That's gone astray. And what is worse
This errant globe was never his.
His good intents for us are curse.

GO TO THE ANT THOU SLUGGARD.... (GK)

As naturalist of some renown,
I own the hunt for clues alone
Would not suffice to hold me long
To search for truth. The joy derived
From nature's splendour found in all -
From tiny ants to landscapes shaped
By fearful forces, or just slow
Imperceptible drip of time -
Delight my eye and fire my mind.
But poets tend to prick balloon
Of pleasure with crass sentiment
That shuns the seeping blood beneath
The beauty. Lyric words cannot
Conceal the brutal facts. With ants
Frenetic lives are ruled by war
That never rests. Thank God they lack
The weapons forged by man! From them

No wisdom can be gained. But still
Their ways decoy my thoughts with weird
Assorted range of forms, all shaped
By ever constant ceaseless strife
That fits each detail to its role.
Relentless march of army ants,
Consuming everything that moves,
Elicits awe. The cunning ants
Who stitch together leaves or farm
A herd of aphids underground
Incite us to investigate.
But only lesson I have learned
Is insight gleaned that, if we still
Persist in mad destructive wars
To settle our disputes, the ants
Are waiting in the wings to claim
This earth for they and their soulless kin.

HISTORY'S LESSONS (TL)

When empires run their course and crack
Or slow implode, as youth protests,
The use of senseless force will speed
Erosion's steady gains until
Exploding rage achieves its aim.
But years of being ruled without
A say have not prepared for aught
But autocratic rule. So soon
A bully seizes reins and once
Again the people's voice is dumb.
External help cannot assist
In ridding world of such unless
The mob itself requests its aid.
This lesson fell on stony ground
With Bush and Blair as they embarked
On folly's move to oust Saddam.

Result is more have died from bombs
And ordnance gone astray and rise
Of irate factions loosed from cage
By which the ousted beast had kept
A peace by means of fear. But now
Unholy mess requires the yanks
Retreat before all hope is blown
Apart as warring cliques are merged
In common front against what's seen
As antigen of foreign threat
That wants to mould and shape their way
Of life, despite the con of well
Intentioned move to give them votes
Before an ordered scene's restored.

HOPELESS CAUSES (TL)

Today we went to church to pause
With thanks for fallen dead in two
Engulfing wars and many times
Our service men, and women too,
Have put their lives on line in cause
Of bringing peace in distant lands.
There's fewer now with medals worn
That bear the head of George the King.
I wear a single silver disc,
With face of youthful Queen, to mark
The time I served in Cyprus when
A rookie lad. Those months had forged
Me into man before I knew
That what was seen as right back then
Had merely slowed the drift to mess
Of fractured land that foolish men
Had not foreseen when launching gang
Of bandits on the scene. Their aim
To force a favoured dream. We'd helped

To save some few from death for time,
But when we'd left for home the new
Regime had failed to keep the peace.
The flood of refugees across
The land, in counterflows, had split
Communities in two. I grieve
For them, as well as for my mates
Who died in hopeless cause. The use
Of death, as means to end, is not
A choice in eyes of Christ, who taught
A special care for those we hate.

IDOLATRY (CO)

Dilemmas jerk the strings in tug
Of war between compassion's claims
And truth's demands. Will call to heed
The cries for justice quell dislike
Of interfering in other's ways?
Will gutless guilt prevail as we
Defer debate? Today the church
Extols the Christ who overthrew
The moneychanger's sordid game,
And yet it tolerates its creeds
And sentimental hymns that shun
Our current knowledge slowly gained
By years of patient toil. We must,
It seems, avoid the risk of hurt
To those who still embrace beliefs
As long outmoded as a dumb
Devotion to astrology's
Ancient untenable beliefs,
Which now we know are merely junk.

We fume, engage in anguished howls,
At folly flowing freely from

Who claim to lead our nation's quest
For peace of which our dreams are made,
As they endorse vile atom bombs
And laser guided missiles aimed
At unreal target bulls. And yet
The tiresome tyrants still prevail.
I find myself aligned with wild
Anarchists and those to whom Christ
Is only man of sense the world
Has known. I own that I still ask
Myself if we alone are off
The rails. And yet the way of raw
Reliance on such godless force
Can only win a war with peace
That's just a thankful pause for breath.
As bills arrive upon the mat,
As simmering resentment once
Again returns, the peace imposed
Becomes but a flimsy gain. The
Ceaseless call to try other ways,
With patient love that Christ commends,
Remains, for world that's ruled by fears,
A recipe too risky for
The worldly wise. Again they'll prove
That arms cannot our ghosts dispel.
Their forms will haunt us still and spawn
Elusive clones of phantom slights
To fuel our foolish worship's praise
Of threats enforced by bully's lame
And feckless strength. In vain I'll weep,
Emit a scream of rage at what
Elected leaders still propose
In all our names. Their wretched polls
Assign me to the left-hand tail
Of con-trick graphs designed to prove
It's what the people want, despite
Deceitful spin of questions asked.

It's not the gormless views of those
Who shun the complex mulish facts
That we should heed. To lead should mean
A fearless nose for what is right
And guts to challenge scorn of those
For whom a slogan substitutes
For thought.   But photo-calls are all
That's offered in reply to cries
 Of 'shame'. The idols still remain.

IGNORANT HUBRIS (TL)

I wonder why it's Islam, built
On faith in God of mercy twinned
With deep compassion, should inspire
Desire among the few who've binned
Koranic texts that make it plain
It's sin to harm a man who can't
Be blamed for what's aroused their hate.
Abuse and violence plainly aren't
Endorsed by sacred book (which once
I read as youth). The Prophet taught
That Jews and those who follow Christ
Are fellow pilgrims, whom he thought
Deserved respect for sharing truth
That only single God exists.
But since the Jews returned to land
Of past their nation state insists
On need to grab a greater share;
Despite it means depriving those
Whose prior claim's beyond dispute.
The guilty West's been led by nose
To only write their protest notes
Alone. When Bush and Blair then go
To war against a Moslem state
It's clear they only overthrow

Islamic tyrant, leaving rest
Distraught, awash with empty words.
In Moslem eyes the West perceives
Themselves as little more than birds
Providing sport for those with guns
Since hunting fox was disallowed.
And as for facts made plain to Blair,
And ever since he's disavowed,
His act of folly made U.K.
Recruiting ground for those enraged
By bombing brother Moslem babes
And mums, who weren't engaged
In acts of terror aimed at West.
If fraction spent on senseless wars
Had been employed in helping poor
Then Bush and Blair would now be blest.

IGNORED (CW)

We sit around a table meant
For meals but now it's laid with piles
Of letters, envelopes and stamps.
We aim to add to heaps of bumf
Augmenting mail that's mainly junk
We throw away each day. Our hope
Is ours will not be so ignored,
For we appeal for worthy cause
In need of funds. Indeed it's those
Who try to raise such money, drop
By drop, who quietly strive to build
A better world. But since the flood
Of like appeals has overreached
The Plimsoll Line of what we can
Afford, we fear that our request
Will enter garbage sack before
The paper knife has disembowelled

It from its sheath. What really irks
Is many rival claims upon
Our ready cash are for research
That taxes should have long supplied.
Instead that gung-ho Bush and Blair
Prefer to pour our nation's wealth
Away to waste of war and stocks
Of weapons only madmen would
Employ in last and final gasp
Before they quit the silenced earth.
They both believe in Christ, they say,
But both ignore his way of peace:
For both rely on force instead.

IMPACT (TL)

We bind your book in finest boards,
Encased with careful, crafted skill,
To standards way beyond the rest.
We feature letters blocked on face
Of finest cloth, a tasteful length
Of ribbon marks your page, a wrap-
-Around and glossy, coloured, dust
Protecting, jacket adds the touch
Of class your work deserves. The price
Reflects the product's way ahead
Of pack impression at a glance.
The words enclosed within are no
Concern of ours, as long as cheque
Is sound. 'Appearance only' rules
Our style of life. You'll understand
Why Tony Blair's our hero still,
Despite the bloody mess he's made
By helping Bush destroy Iraq –
A land of no concern to us
Until we nearly wrapped the wit

And wisdom of Saddam before
Those Yanks destroyed his precious script
In bombing raid upon Baghdad.

INCOMPLETE PICTURE (RE)

A child is painting scene with whole
Attention, like a laser beam
One can't deflect. Her glowing bliss
Is full to brim. The rest of world
Is out of mind. Her self esteem
Is bursting bud as yellows sing
And shapes begin to march across
The page and interact, despite
The fact they've ceased to reproduce
What eye can see. Instead her sense
Of going where her brush demands
She's now embraced, as she explores
A realm beyond what words convey.
She's moved, from wanting picture true
To photo's view, to art that springs
From feelings deep below the calm
Of interface between a pool
And air above on golden days
When wind is taking rest. She's now
Engaged in act of worship, praise
For life, delight in nature's rich
Display and her creative acts
That seem to join in heaven's dance.
It's shame such magic never lasts,
But fades as adult doubting spoils
The vision joy has glimpsed of peace
And harmony that's meant to be.
'Except as child' remains our call.
But Bush and Blair are deaf it seems.
Their yellow bombs just zapped our girl.

INSTEAD (GK)

The latest scare the news inflicts
Affects so few, the risk's so small,
I wonder why they think it's worth
Synthetic fuss. The expert's call
For more research is merely stunt
To get his grant renewed! On way
To work my chance of mishap far
Exceeds the puny odds they say
This novel threat will pose unless
A large amount of public's cash
Is spent at once. Indeed, it's clear
There's urgent need for funds to slash
The rate of deaths from cancer's scourge
And other common ills. Besides
A burning rage engages mind
At thought of Blair who just derides
The many urging monies paid
In tax be spent on finding cures
For dread disease and those deprived
Of means to live. Instead, the lures
Of being seen as leader called
To straighten out the world, has caused
His waste of wealth on arms for wars
In foreign parts. He never paused
To contemplate the deaths and tides
Of hate he'd thus unleash. He's blind
To Gospel's word to use the force
Of love to overcome the mind
Consumed with bitter ire. Instead
His hands, with children's blood, drip red.

INSTEAD OF GUNS (TL)

When woes of world usurp the news
And nearer home a thief has nicked

The lights from bike I'd left beside
The church, I feel that life has tricked
Us all with talk of hope, of peace
And justice won across the globe.
But when a daughter's child pretends
A length of patterned cloth is robe
Of queen, and fancy weaves a scene
In which the right alone prevails,
It's then my spirits lift again.
While much, it seems, is off the rails,
As long as those we love are well
Then life is good. It's when disease
Or hazard causes pain it's then
My mind and soul are not at ease;
And even praying feels it's out
Of tune with what's required to make
Amends. It makes me want to seize
The reins myself, apply the brake,
And turn the human race around
To concentrate resources on
The poor, the sick and those in need:
Instead of guns 'for peace' as con.

IN THEORY ONLY? (TL)

He preaches guru teaching peace
And leaving worldly things behind.
But rage at human folly gets
In way of weak resolve. His mind
Is filled with plots to rid the earth
Of Bush and Blair and other fools
Who worship war as means to ends
Considered good. Whoever rules
Without consent deserves contempt.
But those elected can't be sacked
Until it's time to vote again,

Whatever nation they've attacked
Without assent of public's views
Or UN's code. However long
He rues the day he bought their spin,
To wish them murdered now is wrong.
To wield a knife or pull a gun
He knows he'd shun: and yet he dreams
Of someone else who'll do the deed.
His guru's way's all smoke it seems!

ISRAEL (RE)

The mind goes numb and heart turns cold
At thought of what the Jews went through
As Hitler's hellish plan was put
In place to end a 'race' that gave
And gives the world so much. But now
We're stunned by Zionists who seem
Purblind to deal they've meted out
To those who dwelt within the land
Before the Phoenix Israel rose
Anew. All decent folk must wish
Them well, but not at cost to those
Who want to live in their own home,
From which they've had to flee or been
Expelled. We weep for those who use
The bomb and sniper's random fire
In despairing bid to regain rights.
Their toll of blood postpones return
To ways of justice prophets preached
In distant past. The path to peace
Must be by way of compromise.
Reprisal raids beyond what can
Be justified prevent the wise
From being heard. We pray for sense
To act as yeast within the hearts

Of those whose task it is to lead.
The only god who merits praise
Is Lord of Love embracing all,
Be they Jew or gentile, Copt
Or Arab. Each may call our God
By different name, but He's the same.
His mercy, justice, peace must be
Allowed to reign for good of all.

JUST FOR FUN (TL)

When colleagues formed a singers group
To entertain they chose a mix
Of Tudor hymns and sacred chants
From later years. Their final picks
Were modern, worldly ditties just
For fun. They sang with zest to fill
Our lunchtime break with rare delights.
Their minor flaws and slips of skill
Were masked by pleasure shared amongst
Themselves, and so with us. And yet
It's strange to learn that only some
Believe in God. Do they forget
The Auschwitz guards who fed the fires
By day, with Jews, but relished sounds
Of sacred music after work?
And if this baleful thought astounds
Recall the mayhem caused when fools
Offended Moslems, 'just for fun',
With cartoon showing Prophet armed
With bomb. While I'm prepared to run
With choice of songs performed to please
Alone, there's some who feel unease.

KOSOVO CRUSADE (RE)

As Clintonspeak conspires to numb
Our minds, can soundbites by the men
Of straw revive the dead? Astride
The global stage the shrewd dupes strut,
As NATO proves it always dwelt
Within the realms of make believe.
Can right arrive by missile post?
From thirty thousand feet it's all
A game. The one-armed bandits rule.
Impassioned Blair coyly preens his
New, so Falkland, plumes. His silent praise
Of Thatcher's style belies his claim
To be the hope for future peace.
His P.R. mob can't find the words
To silence carping folk who fume.
The gutter press won't soothe our qualms
With jingoistic piss and slime.
It's time to call the bloody bluff
Of hollow men invoking claim
To be the knights of old. We're bold
To say that bombing kids, and those
Too ill to be involved, is not
The way to oust the evil beast,
Who fans the flames of ancient fears
To keep himself afloat in seas
Of atavistic rage at ills
Of past. To use the naked force
He understands just plays his game.
To kill a single child with bomb
That goes astray condemns us all.
Injustice sprouts from justice dropped
From thirty thousand yellow feet.
May Christ forgive self righteous wrath
That scorns compassion's patient ways.
He went to cross in place of all

Who'd force a man to do their will.
But they prefer the ancient ways.
They claim it's down to earth - despite
The guarantee replenished hate
Will taint the phoney truce achieved,
To fester down the years ahead.
But when the seismic vents erupt
Anew our pundits will be dead.

LAW OF THE JUNGLE (GK)

An enterprise is like a chair
Supported by a set of legs
That number four. The first denotes
The workers' claim to foremost share
Of profits made. Then those who buy
The product should expect a price
That's fair. The state requires at least
Substantial slice of tasty pie
In tax, to fill the public purse
Required to meet our needs for health,
And schools, and all the rest. And last,
From what is left, we may disburse
A dividend to those whose cash
Provided means to build the plant
At start of game. Today, it seems,
Investors jump the queue in smash
And grab that's little short of crime.
But leading band of greedy thugs
Are pension funds, and so we're all
In dock. In irony sublime,
It's only when they're past their prime
The lowly workers get their dime.
And furthermore the public purse
Is robbed to feed the hungry curse
Of senseless wars abroad that nurse

The flames of Moslem's deep unrest
That seeks revenge against the West.
Because of Bush, along with Blair,
Our world's awash with black despair,
As thirst for oil pollutes our air.

'LIBERATED' (CO)

Today the summer drought succumbs
To thunder storms employing guns
In heavy barrage leading rain
That hammers down to quench the thirst
Of dying earth. Relentless fall
Enthralls, as first the puddles form
And then the tiny streams unite
In racing spate that overwhelms
The drains in foaming flood that clears
The trash of weeks of long neglect.
And now the air is clear and all
Is fresh again as grass revives
And hopes return. It's like the days
When war had ceased, ending years
Of tightened belts and nightly fears
Of bombing raids. It's only then
We really drank the joys of peace
And slowly put the pieces back
Again and built our Welfare State.
Today our politicians lack
The knowledge gained by those who learned
The madness war released. The use
Of force to make a point is just
A game for such as Bush and Blair.
But war is never neat. To win
Is only start of problems spawned.
The aftermath is when the task
Of mending broken lives begins.

55

It's also when revenge's seeds
Begin to sprout. To liberate
Each snarling beast in single farce
Will lead to chaos not to peace.
It's no surprise when good intents
Are swept aside by flood of crime
And grumbling cries of those who thought
Their long neglected needs would all
Be fixed as soon as fighting ceased.
Frustrated hopes are worse than bombs
At blowing up simplistic plans.
Besides the people never asked
For foreign troops to help them end
Their freedom's drought they'd borne for years.

MATCH OF THE DAY (CW)

The news reports of war against
Saddam are relished as a sport
To entertain, designed to keep
The ratings high. They bring to mind
The time, some forty years ago,
When I was called to fight against
The terror gangs that Grivas led
In Cyprus, fired by foolish cause
Conveying fear to those who wished
To tend their vines and goats in peace.
We lacked the high-tech means that now
Have turned our TV screens to scenes
Of Sci-Fi nightmare games.
Indeed, we left our heavy guns
Behind on Salisbury Plain, for then
We wouldn't hazard death of child
From faulty aim. Instead we put
Ourselves at risk in constant hunt
On mountain tracks, in narrow streets,

Dispersing seething mobs, in stop
And search of dodgy trucks and cars.
At times our lives were put on line
By planted bombs or ambush tricks.
We could be rough when searching homes
At dawn, but sat the kids upon
·A wall and gave them sweets. Our means
Denied the need to shed a tear
For people felled by random shells
That went astray. Today, it seems,
It's common folk must pay the price.
But I, for one, will have my say -
It's time that Bush and Blair were shipped
Away to distant isle to spend their days
Compiling memoirs full of self
Deceit, for readers just as blind.

March 2003

MISAPPREHENSIONS (TL)

As magma rises from within
He wonders why he feels such rage.
It's not because he knows we've been
Betrayed by Blair. For who'd presage
He'd follow Bush through seas of blood,
Despite 'twas plain the latter bowed
His head to Saudi gods of black
Polluting oil that allowed
Subversive funding's flow without
Restraint to terror gangs around
The globe? The fact that makes him want
To howl is both professed the ground
Of all their folly sprung from faith
In God. But Jesus taught that peace
Requires we treat a rogue as though
He's friend. We'll fail to find release

From war by use of force. Besides
Al-Qaeda claims that each outrage
Is Allah's will to rid the world
Of Islam's foes. To disengage
From weapon worship's false allure
Is what the Way of Christ requires.
But Bush and Blair were caught in web
That thwarted all their good desires.

MISCONSTRUED (TL)

An N.C.O. in charge of foot
Patrol is leading way towards
A rumpus noise across the stream
Dividing ethnic groups by night.
Their peaceful co-existence down
The years has cracked. Fanatics stir
The pot of history's dormant slights.
The Western tribe are restless now
As rumour raises fears. Do shouts
Denote attack is brewing? Soon
The soldiers reach the scene whence sounds
Originate. They quickly learn
The row is fired by feuding pair,
About some cash that's owed. To calm
The crowd the sergeant yells his call
For quiet and asks disputing men
To cease until the day returns.
With grudging nods they move apart
To join their mates. But one, with fist
Aloft, is hurling last abuse.
The sergeant intervenes at speed
And orders silence. Then he turns
Towards the stream on hearing shots.
One ricochets off church. He falls
With arms upraised in crucifix

Display, a bullet through the back
Of head. The ghouls disperse, the old
Departing first and then the young.
A woman weeps beside the corpse
As owl proclaims the sun has set.

MISGUIDED PAIR (TL)

Both Bush and Blair profess belief
In God, but by their acts it seems
They worship Mars and Market Place.
They put their faith in tempting dreams
Of peace enforced by arms and blind,
But footloose, interplay of greeds
And needs to fix a price that's fair
For rich and poor. It's time these creeds
Were laid to rest. For war has yet
To bring a lasting peace. It's just
A pause before resentment stokes
The fires of discontent that must
Erupt anew. The hordes who lose
In fight for share of what they need
To thrive are more than those who win.
We pray fresh leaders will succeed
Misguided pair of good intent.
A worthy end should never use
The gangster's means of getting there.
This duo's deaf to counter views.
Their polished words do not amuse.
They're toddlers wanting lift for swing
From branch of tree but won't accept,
Because of rot, it's bound to fling
Them down in painful fall. Or else
They try to grab a wasp despite
The warning shouts about its sting.
They're wayward kids too sure they're right.

MISLABELLED (CW)

When Gospel came to be the badge
Of state it seems it ceased to be
The guide to inner light. The sword
Was sent upon its way by priests
Who'd missed the Prince of Peace and saw
Themselves as heirs of those who'd blessed
Their warring kings in name of God,
Whose favoured tribe had come to land
From distant Ur. Indeed some popes
Were led astray; for Christ
Had owned no army, nor imposed
His will, nor punished those who failed
To heed his call. His way is love
Alone. Too many rites of church
Were spells designed to keep themselves
From harm. It seems it's always few
Who hear the simple call to be
The yeast of active love within
The dough. The so-called Christian West
Is but a label hiding fact they're last
To make a mark in world that's shaped
By Egypt, Asia, China first
Of all. We're upstart teenage lout
Who thinks the church is ours, despite
It's Asian Christ who slowly tames
Our wild excess and leads us on
To better ways to order lives,
To feed the poor and free the slaves,
In fellowship with those who serve.
It's time our hubris bowed its head.

MISPLACED FAITH? (MC)

A fox is sniffing back and forth
Across our lawn as dawn sets fire

To hem of sky of fleeing cloud.
Its search is hoping for dessert
Before retiring for the day.
My mind is racing to and fro
As theme and words that fit in place
Elude my ceaseless hunt to ease
My angry thoughts at state of world,
Despite belief that God is source
And goal of love beyond the joys
And ambiguities of sex.
Compassion's in decline it seems,
Despite it's only way we know
For justice, peace and hope to thrive.
So why does God withhold his might?
And why not intervene to halt
The terror gangs before their bombs
Are primed? Is freedom such a boon
When children die at hands of those
For whom their cause allows such crimes?
Oh Christ, despite you went to cross
Because by love alone is only way
You conquer hearts, you left the men
Of evil still controlling fates.
Or what is worse, perhaps, it's those
Of good intent who place their faith
In force of arms who still remain.
They urge a care for all and peace,
But then resort to threats of war!

MUDDIED VISION (RE)

Today our nation's in a spin
Regarding European dream.
For some it means a road to peace
And larger market for our goods.
For some it's bureaucratic mire

Impeding individual drive.
For some it's ploy for cutting cord
That makes us dance to tune required
By U.S.A.. It's thus demand
For counterpoise to NATO's weight
Has grown. For some it's seen as chance
To gain the vision France's man
Of blood, Napoleon, espoused;
But lost because he tried to reach
His goal by force of arms. And still
The pygmy men, despite some claims
Of faith in Christ, believe in force
As means of bringing peace to those
Whose legacies of hate erupt
In strife. They never learn that love
Is not imposed, but only comes
As guest when trust has sown its seeds.
Such little men are deaf to Serbs
Advancing case that NATO's war
In Kosovo was crime that needs
To be addressed in court of law.
The danger still is those so sure
Their way is right they cannot hear
The counter claims of sacred doubt.

MUGGED (CW)

His daughter died when drunken yob
Had driven car so fast he'd failed
To take the bend and crossed the line.
At first he'd wept, but long bewailed
His loss of lovely lass he'd loved
From time of wonder birth to day
She'd gained degree in subject long
Desired to make her own. They say
Her talent would have brought success.

But only winsome smile and heart
Of warm compassion now remains
As fading dream. The theft of art
That might have been is minor loss
Compared with joy of watching child
Become a charming woman full
Of life. But rage is more than wild
When I recall the countless mums,
In drenched-in-blood Iraq, compelled
To watch their children slowly die
Because of sanctions that excelled
In being heartless, stupid, all
At odds with facts and sound advice.
But Clinton/Albright, grin endorsed
By Blair, ensured the painful price
Was paid by decent folk oppressed
By Saddam brute that's deaf to dirge
Of sons and daughters, husbands, wives,
Whose mourning cries can never purge
That U.N. sanctioned genocide
On scale to match his own or worse.
The old colonial nations still
Persist in atavistic curse,
When led by self important fools
Who can't conceive they might be wrong.
To add to shame their use of bombs
And missiles made with extra strong,
But toxic, metal causes deaths
From cancers, killing children more
Than most. But later Bush and Blair
Deny the facts and, when to war
Again they go, employ again
Those cancer causing ordnance shown
To gift an aftermath of hell
For friend and foe alike. It's known
Our Western leaders lied as much
As Saddam beast. Their memoirs reek

Of raw deceit without regrets.
My wish for them I dare not speak.
But even worse than those supposed
To work towards a world of peace,
Are crooks who make and sell the arms.
Their profits grow as deaths increase,
Consider cash they loot each day.
It's more than's spent in every year
On search for cures for dread disease
And spinal injured states. It's clear
That money rules their lives, despite
It means my paraplegic son
Can only dream of future cure,
Of being once again to run.
A spokesman claimed their wares are just
As though they'd manufacture knife
That's good for slicing bread or lives.
But bombs have never gifted life.

MY HAT'S INTACT (TL)

She took a thousand photos on
Her trip to blood engorged Iraq.
With artist's eye she now selects
A dozen. Each presents a truly stark
And chilling glimpse, a fleeting look
Of black despair. Compassion stirs
And anger too. How dare our Blair,
With blackguard Bush, whose team defers
To hawkish views from blinkered men
Who worship Genghis Kahn as well
As gravy funds from Zionist Jews,
Presume to interfere. And still we sell
Our lethal arms to Saudi crooks
Who fund fanatic Wahhab youths
Prepared to die in jihads waged

Against the West. But Blair still soothes
With favoured facts that weave a lie.
And when unholy mess results
He still denies his judgement failed.
With sickly smiles he still insults
Our minds. He grins and turns aside,
When questions penetrate the spin
Concealing awkward facts. He acts
As though he's saint who doesn't sin.
I'll eat my hat when Blair retracts.

NAKED FORCE (CW)

They spurn the peaceful calm of lake
Beneath a tranquil summer sky,
As roar of waterfall now drowns
Their thoughts. They hold their hands and gaze
At Siren force, at dance of light
With rainbow which adorns the spray.
For once they stand in awe before
A scene that starts to dwarf their sense
Of selves but seems to lift their souls,
As birds that soar above a mob
Of angry people on a march
Demanding justice, peace and hope.
Can such a flow dislodge the blocks
Impeding minds of those who rule?
Or will the easy fix of war
Postpone the search for lasting peace,
Diverting wrath against a foe
In far off land across the sea?
The lure of mindless force persists.
Desire to ride the waterfall,
To feel at one with awesome will,
Diverts their wish to live their lives
In harmony. They fall for thrills

Of battle seen on films that cut
The pain and loss of feeling heart
That's swept away by naked force.
The righteous sword of tribal god
Usurps the call of God of love.

NO BOUNDARIES (TL)

The babble paused as into hush
A lovely woman entered room.
A shimmer of her silken dress
Reflected dance of silver hair.
Her smile as host received her hand
Was like the lighting of a lamp.
Her grace and charm were soon to put
The shyest at their ease. Her warmth
Was like a day in spring when frosts
Have ceased at last. It seems this glimpse
Of beauty linked to loving heart
Concealed a past in which she'd seen
Her parents killed by Hitler's thugs,
Her sister raped, and brother too,
Before they both were culled. And she
Herself had been abused by beast
Of highest rank, who'd shot himself
When Allies came to liberate
His camp. And now she works with kids
Who've fled the latest war inflamed
By greed and racial hate that slays
Their mums and dads and steals the joys
Of growing up as normal child.
The politicians stay their hands -
A nation's 'free' to bleed itself
To death as long as strife remains
Within its borders drawn by past
Beyond all reason's reach or care.
But she ignores such paltry views.

She quietly reaches helping hand
Across the walls of hate and fear.
Behind her smiles she's forged of steel.

"OBJECTIVE REPORTING" (CW)

As peaceful marchers fill the square
Screaming sirens rend the air
And hated forces of the law
Burst from screen of armoured cars.
Their marksmen shield who wield the clubs,
Herding harmless hungry folk
With blows to skulls and women's breasts
Moving forward like a flow
Of seething lava from a vent.
A teleman is filming all
Keeping clear of faceless troops
And dodging flocks of broken bricks
Bottle splinters graze his hand
As risking life he gets his shots.
Child is hit by ricochet
And at his feet is lying prone.
Lens is turned to drink his pain -
In coloured 'truth' it laps his blood.
Not a hand to tend his hurt
As duty calls for endless frames
Feeding 'facts' to you and I,
While a boy is bleeding cold.
The cameraman receives a prize
For stills that show those pleading eyes,
Which see no more. - Oh Lord forgive.

OFF THE RAILS (CW)

When macho Blair declares we're meant
To lead the way in fighting wild

Fanatic zealots blind to fact
Their dastard means may kill a child
Of fellow Moslem by mistake,
Our counter acts defy all sense
As peaceful passers by are zapped
Along with target gang. Offence
Perceived recruits at least as large
A number bent on swift revenge.
The tit-for-tat of ancient feuds
Is way their fathers would avenge
A bloody raid by foreign tribe.
Today's the same when West decides
To intervene in their affairs.
Unheeding hubris Blair derides
The critics claiming Bush has led
Him on a dance, denies the role
When claiming God informs his mind.
The Way of Christ is set side
When faith in force of arms usurps
His good intents and fears misguide.

ON BRINK (CW)

As spring was showing forth its blooms
We stood on brink of war because
Of Bush and Blair, whose stand against
Saddam was made before they'd shown
The need for haste was justified
In terms of bitter chaos loosed
Beyond the bombs and blood and rings
Of rippling rage throughout the lands
Beyond the battle's scene. The risks
Involved were not assessed apart
From logic they employed to sift
Selected facts perceived through lens
Of Western minds, for whom a match

Between two football teams is seen
As paradigm for most of life.
It's thus they lit a fire that's out
Of hand. Will shifting winds they'd not
Foreseen unwind their tidy plans?
The harvest bombs bequeath, beyond
The tears for children killed when aim
Has gone astray, is rampant weeds
Of discontent and deeply felt
Desire for sweet revenge. The world
Becomes a desert where the ghost
Of reason moans as feelings roam
In fevered frenzy seeking whom
They may destroy, ignoring hordes
Who'd marched against this unwise war.
Until the furies feel they've had
Their fill, we'll have to live amongst
Our shattered pleas and dreams to sift
Amongst the rubble seeking hope
For saner ways to mend the lamps
Allowing light to banish night.
It's blinkered men of good intent
Who've brought us to our present plight.
Until the option war is put
In bin, we'll never cease to sin
By using arms in place of thought
And reaching hands to build the peace.

19th March 2003

ORDERED (CW)

The plums are slowly turning pink,
While apples bide their time as yet.
The leaves are at their deepest green,
As summer slips away to let
The autumn colours sing before

The pause for winter's cold curtails
The dance of life we've just enjoyed.
A thrush is still on hunt for snails
It brings to anvil stone to smash
Apart to relish yielding flesh,
Which builds reserves to see it through
The weeks ahead until, afresh,
The life of spring erupts again.
Then joyous dance of early blooms
Of bulbs we planted months ago
Delights the eye. As distant booms
Disturb the peace, we gaze at clouds
Concealing sun. We watch as bombs
Descend in deadly flocks. We know
Not why. Today the mad pogroms
Are spewed from sky, and not by men
With swords on charging steeds. Before
We saw their eyes of steel; but now
It's screaming planes that kill the poor
From placid heights or missiles fired
By men on ships who've never seen
Our land, our laughing children. "Just
Depress the switch as soon as screen
Displays the cursor's poised to zap
The ordered target on the map!"

OUT OF TUNE (CW)

A wailing wife's a widow now
From latest bomb in market place.
Last week her son was killed by round
From U. S. tank. She cannot face
The thought she's now alone, deprived
Of all for whom she cared. The cant
Of Bush declaring freedom's worth
A little blood ensures her rant

70

Of angry pain denies his claim.
If boot were on the other foot,
And Mrs Bush were killed by bomb
In course of helping him to put
The world aright, I'm sure he'd change
His tune instead of sticking to
His guns by saying loss was worth
The gain. Indeed he's far from true
In claim he follows Christ, the Prince
Of Peace, in all he plans to do
Each day. The Gospel never tries
To force a man to make him new.

OUTSMARTING RISKS? (MC, GK)

It's since that 9/11 crime
That Bush and gang have been hell bent
On showing world its bloodied claws
With constant warning of intent
To crush those nations viewed as threat;
At least those small enough to be
An easy target, so they think.
But since inept attempt to free
Iraq, our lives are now at more
Of risk. And stoking fires of fear
Allows our Tony Blair to shave
Away our freedoms, won so dear.
So simple package from Iran
Is seized as suspect, held despite
The contents clearly labelled 'Tubes
Of insects' and below, and quite
As clear, 'For science only. Treat
With care.' The packet's torn apart,
And contents mixed, before resealed
And sent on way. But sender's smart.
His further samples go to friend

In Turkey. Wrapped anew it clears
The Customs, freed from hijack risk
By those consumed by ersatz fears.

PEACE BREAKERS (TL)

Reports of bombs, of anthrax spores,
Of sanctions killing kids and not
The fiends who rule, of people shot
In error by some rival gangs
For right to peddle drugs this side
Of town, or else a child of ten
Derails a train with concrete block.
Each shock is feeding tide of fear.
Despite these facts, the main increase
Is ghoulish press reporting, on
The hour, of dreadful acts that passed
Us by and never reached our ears
A hundred year ago. Apart
From carnage on our roads, our lives
Are safer now than time we ruled
An empire round the world. Indeed
We're blessed with longer life in which
To seek its meaning, hid at first
By eager youth's desire to make
Its mark or fortune's mirage gains.
But even rogues who've lived a life
Of crime have often found when end's
In sight, they've mellowed as their love
For spouse and children's own erodes
Corroding love of self alone.
Instead of selling arms, it's truths
And values that compassion spawns
Should be our guide, should shape our trade.
Do Blair and Bush desire a war
To turn attention from the mess

They find at home, from death of dreams?
By painting half a dozen states
As black they leave us thinking white
Is colour we possess of right.
They're pair of dangerous clowns with guns
For real they think are merely toys.
When critics point the risks of war
Against Saddam, it's not just death
For mums and babes who get in way;
The powder keg of Arab world
Awaits a clumsy match. But both
Our atavists ignore these fears
That drag the polls away from war.
It's time deluded pair are put
On rocket aimed at Mars, which seems
Is named with just the spin they seek.
Then we can start to cool our fears
And turn our skills to forging peace.

PHONEY PEACE (TL)

Forget uncertain times, a life
That's new and yet unscathed is due!
His heart is filled with love for wife
Awaiting birth they've hoped for long.
We wonder what their lot will be.
Will they have dreams and find that love
Is key? Or will mistaken Blair
And gung-ho gunman Bush bequeath
A phoney peace and constant fear,
Preventing growth of hope for those
Who work to make our world a place
For joy? If only those who lead
Perceived that war is not the way
To deal with those who've run amok.
If only sale of arms were made

A crime. If none would praise the thugs
Whose means to further noble cause
Is terror's way. Perhaps the clash
Of rival views would then become
The subject of debates until
A way is found to reach a pact.
We know these thoughts are fairy land,
But let us try to make them true
By acting all the time as though
They were. It's least we can attempt
As gift to child to be so soon.
Or else we risk this lovely earth
Becoming lifeless as the moon
That's deaf to song, that coldly glides
Amidst the throng of heedless stars.

March 2003

POINTLESS (TL)

Will nation's leaders never learn
That war is seldom worth the gain?
Its wake is stained with debt and hate,
And lives now wrecked by loss and pain.
Its price deprives of means to build
A better world for all until
The coffers fill again. Too soon
Another war ensues. Creative skill
Is then consumed in making arms
And other means of fueling hell
On earth. It's crude inflated fears
That seem to cast an evil spell
Corroding trust, preventing search
For means of building hopes again.
A little aid to bridge the gaps
Is like a longed for fall of rain
When drought has brought despair. The cost

Of giving helping hand is less
Than week of pointless war. Instead
Out leaders play their games of chess
With weapons forged in devil's fire,
Deluding selves the people think
They're macho men of strong resolve.
To most it seems they need a shrink.

POLITICS 2010 (CW)

They bandied bogus figures based
On dodgy mix of facts and guess
At future trends. They hurled abuse
At other side.   They promised more
Than money might allow. 'Twas crude
Attempt to hook your vote, to lure
You into strange belief that they
Alone had key to putting world
Aright. But all's forgot as soon
It's back to mundane minding ship
In storms that money markets make,
Or OPEC boosts with price of black
Resource to keep their profits high
At our expense. They talked about
The need for steady hand to run
The country, blind to fact it's just
The Government they're meant to steer.
The realm still runs itself despite
Their boring spin. But when it came
To making claims for items most
Can not afford they ran amok.
Result was House displayed a crop
Of many new to game. We paused
To see if now they'd vote for what
The country needs. Or would they cling
To stupid view that Britain's beast

That holds its head above the crowd
Of lesser nations lacking scars
Of empire days, and Trident toys,
And placed among the chosen few
Who think they run our complex world?
Investment sharks disdained to think
In terms of nation's good. Defence
Demanded stock of arms we can't
Afford, will never use, but keeps
Afloat the firms who export death
To foreign wars and rotten rogues,
By means of middle men if need
To seem to keep within the law.
Thank God we're free to criticise
And laugh at those who think they rule
Our lives or else to praise who serve.
It's always few who bring disdain
On rest who strive to do their best
To make our land a place of hope
Where justice, care and fairness rule.

PRIORITY PRIORITIES! (GK)

When governments decide to drain
Our tax on arms, including those
We'll never use, atomic bombs
And deadly germs, unless they're mad,
It's then stampede ensues by those
Concerned with urgent needs that raise
A thousand cries for help with funds.
They hammer home their case with mail,
With posters, pleas on internet
And spreads in magazines. Result
Is cake's reduced to crumbs and some
Are left with nowt. Too much research
To find a cure for each disease

Is left to enter fray with cap
In hand, replacing state support
That shares the costs amongst us all.
No wonder people fail to vote
When given chance, as those who win
Inhabit world of spin and place
Their trust in threats of force to keep
The peace. They fail to lead in fight
To build a better life for all,
Except by luring those who can't
Afford the waste of cash that's lost
In Lottery's remotest odds.
Our spirits starve, as nations fail
To strive to cure their poor and sick.
Appeal to trickle down from free
And rampant market place is lie
That's used to justify their con.

PROTEST (CW)

The world of commerce rouses scorn
Within her poet's soul, but how
Our public services would fare
Without the profits trade creates
She doesn't say. To jeer from seats
Beside the track, when race is lost
To rival team, ignores the fact
The winners full deserved the cup.
Her endless jibes at those who hold
The steady jobs that keep the show
Upon the road is just perverse.
Her protest shouts are ultra sounds
Of flea inside the ear of cow
Providing milk. With proper means
One can display the rhythmic tune
And share delight, but most are deaf

To such arcane entreaties fleas
Employ to find their mates. Her words
Are merely screen against a world
She won't engage. In rage at rush
To war by bumbling Blair she joins a march
For peace. But this is only sign
There's nowt that she can do to stop
This farce, that's caused by hasty threat
That time has shown was trap for Bush
From which retreat would spell defeat.
And so the tiger's loosed from cage
Before he knows how far he'll roam
Amongst the restless herds in lands
Beyond his ken. It's time her pen
Applied itself to baser truth,
Exposing use of massive funds
On arms instead of building peace.
Imposing will by naked force
Recruits resentment far and wide
And feeds the need for further arms,
Delighting rogues who sell these means
Of spreading death like AIDS or flu.
It makes me want to favour hell
For faceless men who feed on war.

REACHING OUT (TL)

Today the time devouring spam
Within my e-mail box includes
A screed whose text is jumbled words
In disarray. It makes no sense.
Indeed I wonder why he'd spent
An hour compiling load of junk
To send across the world to self
And other busy folk to no
Avail, except to irritate

On route to trash. Perhaps he lacks
A grain of self esteem and felt
A sense of gain in spewing words
On page to replicate as flocks
Of hungry birds that spread across
The vast expanse of lands and sea
To strangers such as me. Perhaps
The Tower of Babel's only way
To deal with terror ridden times
In aftermath of messed response
By Bush and Blair to dread attack
Of Nine-Eleven's shock. Perhaps
Our hopes for end to war they shunned
Has left us all a wee bit stunned.
Or does it signify we're each
Alone in life without an aim?
Can words no longer serve the end
Of reaching out to other folk,
But merely add to background noise
That fills the voids between the stars?
Not so! There's love of wife and kids,
Delight in theirs so full of life.
But will they learn from our mistakes
Or e-mail fear and hate in rage
At impotence in face of threats
And knee-jerk Government response
Designed to feed the mob's desire
For swift revenge – despite they pour
A truck of petrol on the flames?

RESTRAINT REQUIRED (TL)

When Sid was youth he treated each
And every adult with respect,
Indeed there's some he held in awe.
Today no more does he expect

Response, and let alone regard
For self or fellow O. A. Ps.
Apart from filtered view of past,
It seems the Government agrees.
His neighbour's boy has just been served
With ASBO meant to check his rude
And wilful ways. To him it's just
A badge he wears with pride. His lewd
And noisy talk remains uncurbed.
Is want of self esteem, and lack
Of future jobs apart from drudge
On lowest pay, what drives attack
Against complacent world that's out
Of reach? Is sale of playing field
By Council strapped for cash because
Of Blair's desire to crawl and yield
To Bush's plan to oust Saddam,
Whatever cost in lives or cash?
Are taxes only justified
If used for good and not on rash
And costly schemes that shed the blood
Of children, mothers, cripples, old
And young, when missiles go astray?
As kid did Blair do what he's told?

REWARDING WORK (CO)

A clever lad, who gained a first
And then a Ph. D., proceeds
To postdoc in the States before
He joined a leading team to work
At biomedic cutting edge
Research. But then a firm of drug
Production offered him, for twice
His current wage, a post in lab
With latest gadgets in excess.

But soon he found he's not allowed
To publish all his work. And then
His firm was merged, in secret bid,
With microbe weapons gang that posed
As pesticide research. But since
His earnings hit the roof, he gulped
The bitter pill concealed beneath
This sugared coat. His doubts were quelled.
The boss was paid to deal with those
Who wondered what their work was for,
And how it squared with treaty signed
Some twenty years before. But then
A bright and pretty office girl
Resigned and told the papers all.
A feeding frenzy then ensued.
The shares collapsed. The firm went bust.
He found his record counted nought.
He sold his mansion house and trained
To teach in inner city school.
His bitterness subsided till
He found a deeper sense of gain
In helping kids with little hope
Of building self esteem, to pass
Exams they'd never thought they could.
And he refrained from telling them
About his erstwhile job, or wealth.
Their only clue a gentle wit
Concealing secret cynic's smile.
His former colleagues, who had moved
To other firms, regarded him as crank
And scorned his talk of doing good.

RISKY FREEDOM (MC)

We bought some presents in a shop
And paid by card. The lady asked

For postcode, number only in
Our road, and there on screen our names
Appeared with full address! It seems
Across the world our details can
Be accessed in a trice. It makes
One wonder what the faceless folk,
Who feed the politicians facts
They've filtered with great care, can now
Download on prying VDUs.
Despite the laws, we cannot know
What lies are logged against our names.
And, since those 9/11 planes,
Our grinning leader Blair has set
Aside the need to justify
Arrests without a charge or trial.
We're on the downward slide that ends
With freedom's knell. It's always same
When those of good intent begin
To chip away our hard won rights
In cause of saving us from harm.
It's like those times when fate has dealt
Us days of grief and once again
We rail against our God, who leaves
Us free to run amok instead
Of tweaking strings to keep us all
In narrow paths of righteous ways.
But intermittent exercise
Of might would shackle love with fear.

SCARY (TL)

Our apple tree displays at least
A thousand thousand leaves and yet
A close inspection shows that each
Is not the same as next. To let
The eye perceive them one by one

Reveals a range of size and shape.
The same applies to Chinese hordes
From which the world can not escape,
Despite its fears. But when we've come
To know a few as friends we've found
That each is lovely, one-off, gem.
And furthermore they soon confound
Our views by owning our contempt
For Beijing Party hacks and those
Who rule with fist of steel. We share
A common view when they disclose
Critique of Bush and Blair for wars
Released in Asian lands without
Consent or common sense, or shame
At scary claim they lack all doubt.

SECRET WAR (CW)
(Based on a true incident)

As boy he dreamed of being great,
He'd conquer foes on every front.
His rules would be enforced without
Demur. At school he daily lived
In fiction world inside his head
Or gazed at passers by instead.
He left without a pass in all
Exams he ever sat. And that
You might have thought was that. But no.
He joined the army for a job.
At first it nearly broke his will
As sergeant hounded him to hell.
But soon he's gained a stripe and starts
To learn a leader's not admired,
But feared or else despised. They think
Him fool for choosing extra load
For paltry pay. But now he sees

His sergeant through a different lens.
His heart is ice. He drives his men
From dawn till dusk. He plays the game
By ruthless rulebook's sacred words.
His rigid stance allows no lapse
In petty points of dress. In drill
Perfection must apply. Indeed
He works his men with mean contempt.
With triple stripes at last, he finds
Himself abroad in hunt for thugs
Engaged in terror raids against
The ruling cliques. But still his men
Are treated rough; but then he finds
The impish Ken, who's half his weight,
Is getting laughs at his expense.
In silent fury vengeance now
Erupts. He taunts the lad without
Restraint, beyond all reason's bounds.
At length our Ken retorts one day
'You wait I'll get you in due course'.
A month had passed when ambush fire
Engaged their truck. That day it's Ken
In charge of Bren. So as his mates
And sergeant dive for cover, in
A ditch beside the road, our Ken
Returns the fire of terror gang
And then in pause directs a burst
At sergeant's back before again
Engaging foe on slope above.
At base, inquiry found the brute
Had died from fire of foe, and so
Inform his mum he met his end
In line of duty. No one ranked
Above an N.C.O. had caught
A wisp of truth. When men are trained
To kill they'll use that skill as need
Dictates when tyrant goes too far.
Commissioned ranks are last to know.

SHAME (CW)

The filtered news release distorts
Our view of bloody chaos Bush
And Blair unleashed by stupid war
Against Saddam, and pointless push
To rid Afghanistan of wild
Fanatic creed that's way of life
Since timeless past. A black despair
Descends and living hell is rife
As tribal feuds erupt and crime
Explodes beyond control. The toll
Of mothers killed along with kids
Negates the gain of freedom's poll.
The naked fact's that some who won
A leader's crown are only out
For gains for selves alone. For most
The threats by warlords with the clout
Prevents enforcing measures meant
To make them put away their arms
For good. So rule of law is now
A joke. Despite his Texan charms,
It's clear that Bush has lost the plot.
So saving face is only aim
As second term becomes a farce.
His folly's now his claim to fame.
His talk of hijacked God is sick,
As vested interests shame his name.
His Neo-Cons and Blair's deceits
Destroy our dreams as peace retreats.

SHATTERED (CW)

When Thatcher entered number ten
She quoted words St Francis prayed,
Then swiftly split the nation. So
With Tony Blair the promise came

We'd all unite behind his dreams.
But now simplistic view of world
Affairs has shattered myth, as once
Again we find ourselves at war
Without support of young and old
Who don't believe that things are black
And white. The patient grind we need
To build a peace that lasts is not
For him who wants all targets met
Before it's time to vote again.
The children killed by bombs that go
Astray are just an abstract blip
In figures given spin to show
The press we're sure to win the war.
To build a lasting peace will need
A little more than pious hope
And Western mop for tears and words
Of sham regret for damage done.
His atavistic view that might
Is right belies the faith in Christ
He claims, as Jesus went to cross
Instead of forcing folk to heed
His Kingdom's cause. In death he showed
The lengths that love will go to win
Our free assent. But no, it seems
That Bush is sure his use of death
As friend is way to mould the world
To his design. He truly thinks
The U.S.A. is land of God's
Delight, and he is chosen man
Whose fate's to shape anew our earth
To emulate the dream that Stars
And Stripes have come to symbolize
In place of Kingdom Christ proclaimed,
From healing height and depth of cross.
The lure of mighty dollar rules
Behind the scenes, as polished words

Now flow with actor's ease, despite
Their hollow ring and stench of pride.

March 2003

SHATTERED DREAMS (RE)

As terror gang outrages world
Again, by shedding blood of those
They've never met or known by name,
The politicians scream revenge.
Elusive prey evades their bombs
And troops with hate renewed. Unless
The cause of anger's fire is put
To rest they'll strike again. Their rage
Is cloaked in copy filched from words
They learned in mosque while missing truth
That God denounces war. Too much they learned
By rote without engaging mind.
Their hearts were fed on hurts perceived
But not addressed by those they see
As foes. Despair is food that feeds
Their disregard of pain and tears
They cause to those who wish, like them,
For world of justice, peace and hope
For all alike. While those who sell
The guns and like are pleased to see
Their markets ever grow. Their greed
For profit far exceeds the sins
Of those who offer death as way
To mend their shattered dreams and lives.
Their cause is just, their means are vile.
But would I hold to such a view
If I were in their painful shoes?
Oh God we merely wish for world
That's safe for children now and when
They're grown enough to have their own.

SNOOKERED (RE)

Enraged by news on tele screen,
He downs his pint in single draught.
'I tell you true' he says to mate
'It makes me want to snooker sods
Who think they're gods, despite the fact
They're only yobs the mob elects
To legislate for good or ill.
Just ken the mess they've made of things;
Diverting money, meant to aid
The growth of justice, peace and health,
To wars in foreign parts: to please
Them Yanks. They've made our world a place
Of greater danger, fear and risk.
This Bush and Blair are just a pair
Of goons. They fancy eggs are meant
For playing snooker redesigned
With balls to match those used by men
Who won the rugby football cup
When policies, that failed, required
Diverting spin to help us all
To overlook the shit we're in.
I tell you mate we shan't forget
When time for ballot comes again!'
His friend ripostes 'Ignore the fools!
They're only fit for breaking rules
Of common sense they lose as soon
As grubby hands control the gears
Of State machine. So cool your fires
Of fury, order round of drinks,
Then shoot them balls, or lose the frame!'.

SOMALIA 2011 (TL)

They'd fled from drought and civil war
With little hope and less to eat.

With baby boy and older girl
Forever growing weak, they sipped
From precious water in a can,
But not enough to slake their thirst.
They'd walked for seven weeks, beneath
Relentless sun, before they reached
A U. N. camp. Too late. Their boy
Did not respond to tender care
And slowly turned his pleading eyes
To those of mum and sighed, then died.
Her girl began a slow return
To better health, but dad now took
A turn for worse when fever struck.
Despite the best of care it came
To late. He's laid to rest beside
His son. A fool imam declared
It all was Allah's will, although
That meant their deaths were part of plan,
And sin of man was not to blame.
If that were so then God's malign.
But no! Our Father God is love,
And source of same in hearts of man.
We live in world of chance and choice.
Afflictions spring from nature's whims
And sin. Whatever cards are dealt
By either means embrace of God
Will give us strength, or ease our moves
Beyond our graves. Emergent souls
From selfish beasts, from which we came,
Is what our lives are all about.
The choice is ours. The grace of God
Awaits our smallest cry for aid.
Despair of mum and dadless girl
Reminds us Christ, who died on cross
And shared our pain, arose from tomb.
And now He helps us walk His way
Of loving service, joyful hope.

Whatever hazards hinder, God
Will never cease to help us cope
Or else receive our souls instead.

STATUES (RE)

The Polish Pope is keen on 'saints'.
Indeed he's added more than all
Who've reigned before. His church is ship
Of quaint design. It's weathered wars
And many storms. Its listing load
Of ballast misfits trimmed by gold
Of cargo, muddles saints along
With sinners too. But who can sort
The sheep from goats when inner selves
Are what we need to weigh? At least
His candidates must die to get
On list; as nations free and fair
Who only place their leaders on
A plinth when they are dead: but when
A state is ruled by fist of steel
The image seen in every town
Is bronze of boss – until he's died
Or pushed aside. So when some clowns
Approved a statue, while she's still
Alive, of saintéd Thatcher in
Their eyes, a vandal rightly lopped
Its head. A greater sin was when
The Yanks could not refrain from task
Of felling Saddam's artless bronze
Before Iraquis claimed their right
To do the job themselves. The best
Of effigies I've seen are those
Of nameless common soldiers sent
To war because of feuds between
The fools who failed to opt for peace.

STOKING (TL)

His surface calm, his shy but kind
And helpful ways conceal a rage
Within. He knows the second rate
Have stolen credit due to him:
But he'll not stoop to showing signs
He cares a jot. He feels content
His patient work has paid returns.
For him the search is game that counts.
Perhaps it's thrill of chase that still
Survives in brain from times
When mankind lived in caves. For now
He craves a world devoid of war,
Where hoodlums, such as Bush, are banned.
To put one's faith in force has long
Been known to fail. Indeed it makes
It worse by stoking up the fires
Of bitter sweet revenge that bides
Its time with patient scheming plots
Of pure surprise. Unless the cause
Of hate and seething ire are sought
And then embraced by real attempts
To find a cure, the pain will grow
And fester out of sight before
Erupting when we least expect.
The Romans failed to learn this truth,
And still the men of power remain
Immune. Sharon and ilk are still
In place as letting blood persists
As only mad response employed,
Despite it builds a head of steam.

THE FEUD (TL)

An overhanging bough excludes
The sun from favoured plants below.

With bow saw working smoothly clean
It's quickly lopped. But, as I slice
It into logs for friend along
The road, I start to think of men
Of old who felled a tree with ax
Of stone all tightly bound with thongs
Of leather into haft of piece
Of branch that caught the eye for shape
That fitted need. For them the speed
With which my job is done would sure
Amaze. The reach of progress still
Continues, shrinking tasks that once
Consumed the hours, allowing dreams
To be the norm. But still we lack
The wisdom living side by side
With diverse folk requires for peace
To reign. Removing straying bough
Of neighbour's tree once started fight,
Despite the law that made it clear
Which side was right. Their silly war
Engulfed their street, whose rival camps
Were spitting cats who'd soon forgot
The cause of feud that carried on
For years beyond when pair had moved.
It struck me Ulster's like that street.

THE GULF (TL)

In war against the terror gangs,
The cowboy Bush has overlooked the crimes
Of those who aid his cause. A thug
Who lets supplies to U.S. troops
Be trucked across his land ignores
The human rights of those who claim
He's plain corrupt. They're locked in jail,
They're tortured day by day and two

Are boiled alive. When Bush is told
These truths, by C.I.A., he shrugs
The charge aside for fear the flow
He needs will cease. Synthetic smiles
Are used to silence those who probe.
He deftly dodges questions aimed
By those who've found a trail of facts
Exposing cover ups and lies.
He pleads his moral cause without
A blush. It brings to mind the days
Before the Iron Curtain ripped,
When Russian leaders made an art
Of moulding news to fit the view
They wished to sell, despite the gulf
Between their tales and what was real.
Indeed, like them it seems that Bush
Desires to show the world that way
Of jungle's fine as long as U.
S.A. is tiger king who wears
The sheriff's star without restraint
Of rights of those beyond his patch.
It's time to run him out of town.

THE THREAT (RE)

Today the major threat to peace
Is Bush and Blair intent on war
To oust the beast from Baghdad's scene.
To them the world's a Western film
In which their role is crystal clear.
They'll rid the joint of pesky scum.
They'll ride the outlawed bum from town.
They're deaf to those who rightly say
"Beware the strutting brute who huffs
And puffs, he'll spit with fire and blood
If cornered, back to wall. It's then

You'll see his crimes to date are just
A playground bully's game. He'll bring
The building crashing down as, hand
In hand with death, he'll wreak revenge".
Instead of war we need to walk
The road to peace for all within
The Middle East. We need the Jews
To recognise the rights of those
Whose land they've seized. Delete
The source of anger keeping pot
On constant boil. Sharon and beast
Are both at risk of sparking war
Engulfing much of world and more.
Both Bush and Blair declare belief
In God of peace, but place their faith
In fiendish instruments of death
Instead. Their deeds not words will lift
The lid on what they worship deep
Within their hearts and minds.
Their atavistic stance is far
From being sane. It's pure inane.

THUGGERY (CW)

A brawling kid was beaten hard
By dad who wielded leather belt.
Result his son is now a thug.
When Bush and Blair had chosen war
To oust Saddam they opened cage
Releasing savage beasts athirst
For blood, consumed with rage, as death
Prevails and mothers mourn. There's lack
Of signs of peace and justice meant
To be the gift of pair of fools
Who think they're called by God to be
The means of building Kingdom Christ

Proclaimed is only made from bricks
Of love, each gently laid and sealed
With mercy one by one until
All hate has died away for good.
But no, they're hooked on tribal god
Whose righteous wrath demands revenge
And sacrifice appeasing ire
At lack of zeal. They cannot see
The cross has signalled end of all
Such atavistic ways, condemned
The use of force to gain one's ends.
A war in name of righteous aim
Is oxymoron clad in spin.
Indeed is greater sin than gang
Of thugs who mug a crippled man.

TIME BOMB (TL)

To be alive today we're blessed
With lots that's good and much to ease
The grind of daily chores. The news
Ensures we hear the crying pleas
Of those in need of aid, so more
Respond than in the past. Instead
Of war we could provide each child
With all their meals and bed
To sleep each night. We squander cash
On arms for fights we could avoid
Or sell them over internet
To gangs of thugs. So null and void
Are windy words about the aid
We proudly tell the world we give.
It's merely crumbs we can afford.
I doubt the future will forgive
The seeds of conflict sown by those
Who trust in force to deal with rage

Of those who feel deprived of right
To share in wealth of present age.

TOXIC MEANS (TL)

As war on weeds begins, as spring's
Display of daffodils delights,
My thoughts astray recall our troops
At risk in far Iraq. When Bush
And Blair dispatched them there they'd hoped
To win an easy ride across
A land awaiting freedom's joy.
But many only felt enraged
At foreign troops, resenting bombs
That went adrift to kill or maim
Their kids and wives. They truly wished
To rid themselves of Saddam's rule,
But not at cost of many lives.
These interfering Western hordes
Are like a poison spray that kills
The crop along with pests. It's why
I slowly gather slugs and snails
By hand, avoiding toxic means
Bequeathing tempting meal to give
A thrush a stomach pain or worse.
Our fighting men are not to blame
For havoc handed out from tank
And plane. It's Bush who wanted war
To show the world who's boss as soon
As nine eleven's mess had been
Removed and anger over loss
Of life and pride had simmered down.
The marchers who opposed his war
Were only bleeding hearts he could
Ignore, but when the president
Of France began his cynic's game,

All dressed in flimsy garb of pure
Deceit, his patience snapped. It's bombs
Away before a wiser voice
Could have its say. It's thus the world
Today is stalked by fear and hate.
The cause of peace awaits the kiss
Of life – from whom we do not know.

TRIBALISM (TL)

Our lawn is hunting ground for pair
Of blackbirds nesting in the hedge.
Each morning tardy worms are plucked
From earth's embrace. But soon from edge
Of roof a gang of starlings swoop
To scour this private patch without
So much as by their leave. The same
Applies to playground when we're out
With grandchild on a swing and horde
Of teenage kids appears and runs
Amok and scares the tiny tots.
But in Iraq it's men with guns
And homemade bombs. They ruin peace
For people just concerned with work
And raising children undisturbed
By foreign thugs, or native jerk
Who robs the poor without constraint
Of conscience now curtailed, as long
As victim's from another sect.
Does Islam not condemn their wrong?

TWO DADS (TL)

His dad was drunk for most of time.
His mum was much abused. His mates
Had likewise had it rough. Indeed

They're tough and sure defend themselves
And friends against attacks that might
Encroach upon their patch. He'd had
His knocks and fun with girls.
Beneath his hardened shell his heart
Was kind. But still his world was black
Or white. It's us or them. And so
He joined the army soon as age
Allowed. They'd tamed his will a mite,
Like breaking in a horse. But still
He's looking for a fight. At last
He's posted overseas to play
His part in war against a gang
Of thugs who'd launched a terror plan
To thwart the work on dam for which
Their land was grabbed by those who ruled.
He relished chance to hone his skills
At killing foes he's told are bad.
It's only when he falls for lass
He met in bar he starts to see
The cause, of those opposed to those
For whom he wages war, is just.
Her dad had farmed a piece of land
That he'd had seized. The sum they paid
Would only feed his wife and child
For half a year. So in despair
He joins the party who obstruct
The dam. In protest march he's hit
By plastic bullet in his eye,
Which lost its sight. At first he raged
At daughter's choice of our man Jack.
But soon he sees they're deep in tide
Of passion's flood and Jack has lost
His taste for fight. He buys discharge
And weds his lovely lass. And soon
He joins the party of her dad.
So now he's wanted man on list

Of former mates, who think
He's traitor fit for early grave.
His special knowledge of their ways
Is greatest gift to new dad's cause.

UNEDUCATED SCHOLAR (CW)

A throwback classics don perceives
Himself as being raised above
The herd. The admin staff he treats
With blatant curt disdain. His love
Of self is only love he owns,
Apart from books on ancient Rome.
He's blind to nasty facts behind
Its ordered state. His weighty tome
Selected data most admired;
Ignoring legions' trampling feet
And bloody swords, the role of slaves
Supporting plebs and rich elite.
What makes him think that he'd have been
A part of cream, and not a slave
Whose master drove him hard from dawn
Till dusk, and thus to early grave?
His hubris mien has made him blind
To low esteem with which he's viewed
By those who ease his shielded life
That seems to most so sadly skewed.
Because the Christian dogmas learned
As child had failed to feed his dreams,
He'd pulled the plug, discarding gift
Of Gospel love that still redeems
Despite attempts to codify
Its sacred fire and thus restrain
Its all renewing flame. Instead
He'd looked to ancient Rome's domain
For guide for life, thus turning back

On modern times and losing track.
Today he's unknown scholar hack
Whose unread book's in basement rack.

UPSTARTS

When Gospel came to be the badge
Of state it seems it ceased to be
The guide to inner light. The sword
Was sent upon its way by priests
Who'd missed the Prince of Peace and saw
Themselves as heirs to those who blessed
The warring kings in name of God,
Whose favoured tribe had come to land
From distant Ur. Indeed some popes
Were led astray; for Christ
Had owned no army, nor imposed
His will, nor punished those who failed
To heed his call. His way is love
Alone. Too many rites of church
Were spells designed to keep themselves
From harm. It seems it's always few
Who hear the simple call to be
The yeast of active love within
The dough. The so-called Christian West
Is but a label hiding fact they're last
To make a mark in world that's shaped
By Egypt, Asia, China first
Of all. We're upstart teenage lout
Who thinks the church is ours, despite
It's Asian Christ who slowly tames
Our wild excess and leads us on
To better ways to order lives,
To feed the poor and free the slaves,
In fellowship with those who serve.
It's time our hubris bowed its head.

WAR (RE)

She tabled sheets of stocks and sales,
And profit/loss per items sold,
All neatly ranged in ranks and rows.
She then observed, with false lament,
Our prices need to be increased.
But softly spoken man, she thought
Of little worth, addressed the chair.
He quietly undermined the sums
Per units shown, revealing flaws
In underlying bases used
That varied right across the spread.
The rustled papers, scratch of heads
Of others right and left, now showed
They'd not considered figures thus.
The chairman gave assent to view
We need the facts, not lies, before
Decisions can be made. And so
Reprieve achieved for time a chance
To put a rival case. But she
Who'd fudged accounts was boiling mad
With anger's hidden rage. She smiled
At one and all and pleaded weight
Of work had led to minor faults
In database she'd used in haste.
Beneath synthetic charm she seethed
At loss of face and vowed revenge.
It's thus a secret war began.
It's thus that nations find themselves
In clash of arms without a cause
That merits killing mums and kids.

WAR ON WAR (TL)

Unless we cease to honour men
Whose use of war to force their will

Is only skill that they possess,
We'll lead the young astray. Today
We need to trash the toys and films
Suggesting war is natural way
To settle our disputes.

And as for those who trade in arms
They should be banished now for good,
Along with those who scream revenge
For minor slights. To fight is last
Resort when other efforts fail
To bring us peace. And even then
It's matter for regret.

Unless we seek to undermine
The view that war is normal means
That's justified when evil looms
And threatens peace, we'll shun attempts
To settle matters causing ire
By civil talks. We'll thus condone
The pointless death of child.

To feign surprise and sorrow's mask
When children die by accident
Of bombs that go astray is cant
That should be made a crime. Both Bush
And Blair should face a judge for blood
They've spilled without intent to maim
Or kill the innocent.

'WE REGRET...' (RE)

Enraged by ceaseless whine at night
Mosquitoes made, he bought himself
A pistol, poured a glass of rum
And sat in wait. He zapped a few

At first: but as his drink was downed
His aim began to drift. A vase
Was split apart, a mirror smashed,
A bottle shattered too. But still
Those thirsty gnats destroyed his peace.
At least it's not as bad as time
He tried to kill a cockroach horde
Behind his fridge. He'd used a bait
Of poisoned bran with great success,
Until his favoured cat had tried
It too and died in pain. Today it's Bush
Who shoots from hip without regard
For risks to those who share his wish
To rid their land of vermin's blight.
His sanctioned use of cluster bombs
Has left a swarm of bomblets just
Awaiting children unaware
They're still alive. Now hundreds die
Or lie abed, each maimed for life.
Perverted minds must first conceive,
Or coldly order, such device.
The lesson Dresden's plight has left
As stain on history's page remains
Ignored. We still employ excess
Of force to swat unwelcome pests.
We still are using gun for gnats.

WITHOUT A DOUBT (CO)

It's said that Bush believes that God
Endorsed his rush to war to oust
Saddam. I've trawled the text
Of Gospels, one by one, and met
A' man of peace who shuns the use
Of force. Besides he'd learned in youth
Of tribal Lord of Hosts in scrolls

That date from times before the Jews
Began to learn that God was not
Their private weapon in reserve.
As man he taught - you've heard of old
An eye for eye, but I declare
To follow me is way of love:
Revenge is not my choice when cheek
Is struck by bloke in fevered rage.
It seems that deafness won that day.
It seems that Bush is likewise deaf
To those who don't believe that God
Regards the U.S.A. as land
He chose to be his Kingdom's key.
The Holy Spirit works away
Behind the scenes in hearts of those
Who shun display but quietly strive
To serve the cause of peace with care
And patient ear. When doubts assail
They learn in retrospect to hear
The words of comfort clear. Unless
One senses Bush has fought the fear
He might be wrong we'll treat him as
Saddam, who huffs and puffs until
As cornered yellow kid he quits,
But leaves a legacy of hate
To smoulder down the years to come.

WORLD TRADE CENTER (CO)
11th September 2001

When chilled fanatics flew those planes
To sudden death for them, for those
On board and thousands unaware
Their days on earth were done, the world
Was stunned. Heroic rescue work
Redeemed a gleam of hope. But soon

The media swamped us all in flood
Of relished scenes and pundits, whose
Recycled, cliché ridden, views
Became a steady chant for crude
Revenge by means of war. The rage
Aroused soon stifles wiser words
From being heard. Unless the cause
That drove those men to kill themselves,
In balls of screaming fire, is seen
As howl of anguish wrung from pit
Of bleak despair, we'll merely reap
A steady harvest of the dead.

But who am I detached from scene?
Across the seas, in comfort, I'm
Remote from flames; despite the fact
That in my youth a pair of bombs,
A terror gang had placed in tent
Across the way from me and mates,
Impaired my hearing to this day;
Despite the fact my wife was dug
From choking dust and dark remains
Of home destroyed by Nazi bomb;
We're merely distant ghouls at rim
Of hell. It's hard to comprehend.
My daily routine hasn't changed.
I wrestle problems as before,
Researching flies, in work that seems
To most divorced from daily life.
It makes one wonder if one's sane.
And yet it's clear I have a flair
For culling yields from tiny field
Of scholarship. Besides, most tasks
Are done to aid a colleague clinch
A puzzle, advise about a pest
Abroad, or help police to solve
A crime. At times I seem denied

The hours to work on projects I
Desire to do before I die.

When I review the varied lives
Of scuttle flies I'm filled with awe,
In sense of wonder and of fear.
I'm glad I'm not an ant who's slow
Consumed by maggot feeding on
My non-essential organs first,
Before it eats my brain, and then
Employs my empty shell of head
As shelter for its pupal pause
Before the fly is born to hunt
Another ant in turn. The pain
And death these tiny flies dispense,
In human terms, reflects the vile
Effects of those consumed by hate.

They flew those planes with grim intent
To further cause, to kill and wound
Whose names and loves and lives remained
Of no concern. Their mates rejoice
As outraged headlines scream revenge.
Their cold indifference, to death
Of infants, husbands, wives and those
Whose duty is to help the maimed,
Erodes the urge to heed the hurts
And ills that they perceived as spur
To act with such disdain against
Those helpless folk whose daily wish
Was peace. As long as violent means
Are used by those in power, blood
Is spilled by those denied all hope
Of better lives. No interchange
Of views prevails in search for rights
And justice in our time. For hate
Is like a maggot eating first

The feeling heart, until the head
Is deaf to reason's cries for calm
Reflection on the way to reach
The promised land of common good.
Instead revenge prevails and death
Is laughing at its cheap success
In ceaseless cycle of despair.

WRONGLY ARRESTED (TL)

We wonder why she signed for course
For first degree. It seems perhaps
Her choice was merely what her friend
Had opted for. Or else a lapse
When filling in the form. Result
Is unexpected first in what
The ancient Arabs wrote and thought.
Her plumber dad declared it rot
And asked her what she had in mind
For getting job to pay for bread, for tax
And all the rest. She shrugged and gave
Her dad a knowing look. 'Relax'
She said 'I will survive'. But in
The night she worried wild and long
As credit crunch began to bite.
By day her heart's devoid of song,
As filling shelves in local branch
Of grocer chain was all the work
She'd found. Her dream of scholar's life
Had died. Her task began to irk
Beyond her Plimsoll Line of what
Her mind would tolerate. Too soon
She sought escape in drink, before
A dodgy friend in low saloon
Cajoled her into trying dose
Of stronger drug. She soon was hooked.

But dad was so concerned he asked
Police to stop her, get her booked
For having drugs, and give her choice
Of treatment or a charge and fine.
At first she's mad with dad. Indeed
She'd turn away and would decline
To give reply when asked about
Her therapist. But now she's glad
He interfered, as back on rails
Again she knows he wasn't bad.
He'd merely, out of love, had felt
Obliged to act to bring her round
To sense. Instead of scholar's life
She's now employed to help expound
In Arabic when Moslem lads
Are facing law as suspects lured
To wanting way of sweet revenge
Against the likes of Blair, cocksured
As fellow fool the younger Bush.
When both attacked Iraq, along
With other blunder acts throughout
The Moslem world, the rage at wrong
Was bound to stir the wrath of young
Of Islam's faith. They too belong
To diverse British scene, where all
Are free to think apart from throng.
But most have no desire to use
The bomb to make their feelings known.
Besides in thinking Bush and Blair
Were reckless crooks they're not alone!

WRONG TARGETS (TL)

A local centre helping youths
In need of help with mental health
Is starved of funds because its grant

From NHS has ceased. Our wealth,
Purloined as tax, is used instead
To zap Iraquis. Never mind
They're mostly not the ones our bombs
Were meant to hit. For Blair is blind
To naked facts his foreign wars
Have made our world a place where men
Of violence thrive and seek to wreak
Revenge. At home by age of ten
Our schools, by many tests, have sieved
The able from the rest. Among
The latter some have lost their self
Esteem, their sense of worth. They're flung
Aside, it seems. Their shattered dreams
Induce resentment's need to show
The world they'll fight to gain respect
That's based on fear. A random blow
Against the better off is how
They gain a thrill. Of this I'm made
Aware when traffic cones are hurled
At self when riding by at staid
And steady pace on bike without
A glance at gang of youths beside
A stretch of road repairs. My rage
Is held in check. As I outride
A running yob, I wonder what
Would rectify his moral rot.

Collections of Poems
By Henry Disney

FM - FINDING MYSELF (Outposts Publications, 1963 - 20 pages).

QUESTINGS (Chester House Publications, 1982 - 54 pages)

LAPSED ATHEIST and other poems Rockingham Press, 1995 - 40 pages).

COUNTERPOISE (Ronald Lambert Publications, 2004 - 171 pages) A MUSING COG (Ronald Lambert Publications, 2006 - 125 pages)

"GUIDED BY KNOWLEDGE, INSPIRED BY LOVE" (Eloquent Books, New York, 2009 - 193 pages hardback edition)   Pneuma Springs Publishing, UK, 2014 – 168 pages, paperback edition). Also available on KINDLE

REITERATION (Pneuma Springs Publishing, UK, 2011 - 151 pages). Also available on KINDLE

'TEACH US OF LOVE' (Pneuma Springs Publishing, UK, 2012 - 273 pages). Also available on KINDLE

COME WHAT MAY (Pneuma Springs Publishing, UK, 2014 – 308 pages).

About the Poet

Henry Disney was born in Dorset in 1938. From the age of 3-7 the War resulted in himself and two sisters being separated from their parents, who were stuck in the Sudan. On leaving school in 1957 he did his National Service in the Royal Artillery, becoming a bombardier on active service in Cyprus before becoming a subaltern on Salisbury Plain. He then read Natural Sciences at Cambridge University (with a part I in zoology, botany and geology and a part II in zoology). He was then Assistant Warden of the Flatford Mill Field Centre in Suffolk, mainly teaching field zoology. On marrying the Centre's secretary, Audrey, they were obliged to leave for a lack of married accommodation. He was then the Medical Entomologist at the Dermal Leishmaniasis Research Unit in British Honduras (Belize), employed by the Ministry of Overseas Development. His research was mainly on the ecology of sandflies (Phlebotominae) and mammals in relation to a parasitic infection contracted by people working in the rainforest. He returned to Bristol University to study for a Certificate in Education. He then joined the Overseas Staff of the Medical Research Council as the Medical Entomologist at the Helminthisasis Research Unit in Cameroon. His work was mainly on the ecology of blackflies (Simuliidae) in relation to river blindness (Onchocerciasis). Having produced three children, each born on a different continent, he and Audrey returned to Britain; where from 1971-1984 he was Director of the Field Centre and National Nature Reserve at Malham Tarn in North Yorkshire. He also carried out research on the natural history and taxonomy of flies (Diptera); mainly on meniscus midges (Dixidae) and scuttle flies (Phoridae). From 1984-1998 he was the Field Studies Council Research Fellow in the Department of Zoology of Cambridge University, primarily researching the natural history and taxonomy of the scuttle flies of the world. Following his 60th birthday he was forced into early retirement by a lack of Research Council support for insect taxonomy, despite Cambridge University having awarded him both a Doctor of Philosophy degree and a Doctor of Science degree for his published contributions to our knowledge of Diptera. He continues his research on the natural history, taxonomy and evolution of world scuttle flies at Cambridge University's Department of Zoology.

Apart from the above sketch of his formal curriculum vitae, he has been involved in other activities. These include being co-founder and co-editor, with Dr Sally Corbet, of the acclaimed Naturalists' Handbooks series, serving as a Ministerial Appointee on the Yorkshire Dales National Park Committee, serving on the World Health Organisation's Scientific Working Group on Filiariasis and on their Advisory Panel for the Onchocerciasis Control Programme, being an adviser to the Sri Lankan Ministry of Education on their field centre programme, being a Governor of Kirkby Malham Primary School, being a churchwarden of the parish of Kirkby Malham, and at the Church of the Good Shepherd in Cambridge, being a Pastoral Selector for the Anglican Church's Advisory Board of Ministry; being a participant in the Royal Entomological Society's Project Wallace expedition to Sulawesi in 1985; and being a Director of Dervish Mine Clearance Limited (concerned with clearing antipersonnel landmines). Otherwise, and (according to him) far more important than all the above, he is a widower (formerly husband of Audrey, who died the year before their golden wedding), father and grandfather.

Other book(s) by Henry Disney

REITERATION
Mobi eISBN: 9781907728969
ePub eISBN: 9781782281603
PDF eBook eISBN: 9781782280804
Paperback ISBN: 9781907728143

'Teach us of Love'
Mobi eISBN: 9781782282457
ePub eISBN: 9781782282341
PDF eBook eISBN: 9781782282563
Paperback ISBN: 9781782281849

Come What May
Mobi eISBN: 9781782283362
ePub eISBN: 9781782283393
PDF eBook eISBN: 9781782283423
Paperback ISBN: 9781782283331

Guided by Knowledge, Inspired by Love
Mobi eISBN: 9781782283775
ePub eISBN: 9781782283799
PDF eBook eISBN: 9781782283812
Paperback ISBN: 9781782283751
Book(s) by Henry Disney

REITERATION ISBN: 9781907728143
REITERATION covers the poet's varied experiences from his active service in Cyprus in his youth, being a medical entomologist in the tropics, his Christian faith, political observations, scientific insights and being a husband, father and grandfather.
A reviewer of his previous poems says "Henry Disney's is... a beautiful mind, and a tough mind"

Teach us of Love ISBN: 9781782281849
"Henry Disney's is, to borrow a phrase, a beautiful mind, and also a tough mind." So wrote Kitty Ferguson in her review of his sixth

collection. This eighth collection of poems reinforces this perception.

The topics covered reflect varied experience, distinguished contributions to science and a deep commitment to Christian values and perceptions.

Come What May ISBN: 9781782283331
Henry Disney is a distinguished scientist (who has worked in tropical rainforests, the Yorkshire Pennines and Cambridge University). While employing regular metre and rhyme he is a thoroughly modern poet of deep insight and compassion combined with acute observation and a critical mind. These highly readable poems repay reading again and again.

Guided by Knowledge, Inspired by Love ISBN 9781782283751
First published in New York in 2009 for the Darwin bicentenary, as many Americans reject the theory of evolution, despite convincing new evidence, especially molecular evidence, since Darwin. Compelling witness to the harmonious relations between science and religion is in the lives of scientists who are also Christians. Henry Disney is both.

Lightning Source UK Ltd.
Milton Keynes UK
UKOW02f1257280715

255953UK00001B/14/P